MW01233900

Healing Arts Publishing
A Division of *The Worldwide Center*
Evergreen, Colorado

The Simple Truth
About God

by Christine Lenick

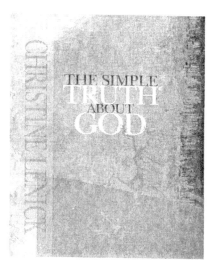

Other Healing Arts Publishing Books
Healing Through Love
by Marilyn Innerfeld

The above titles are available at your local
bookstore. Copies may also be ordered at *The Worldwide
Center* website **www.expandedliving.net** or by calling
303-674-7704.

Healing Arts Publishing
The Worldwide Center for the Healing Arts, LLC
P.O. Box 4223
Evergreen, CO 80437

Visit our website at www.expandedliving.net

Printed in the United States of America.

ISBN: 0-9711522-6-8
LC: 2003103385

Cover and Interior Design by
Michele Renée Ledoux
michele@mledoux.com | www.mledoux.com

This book is available at quantity discounts for
bulk purchases. For information, call 303-674-7704.

This book is dedicated to
the friends of my heart across lifetimes.

Contents

Appreciation

This book is the outgrowth of an unusual experience that occurred in the fall of 1998 and continues today. This experience has been shared most closely with three friends and soul mates: my husband Ben; my lifelong friend, Diane; and one of my very essence, Marilyn Innerfeld.

On these pages, I share with you the depths of my appreciation and love for these three soul mates, for without their love and guidance, the experience as ours and mine would not have been as it was.

To my loving husband, I give my heart for his unconditional acceptance and celebration of me. He has traveled with me as my companion in each moment, never questioning, only accepting openly that my experience was extraordinary. He is extraordinary. Our love is forever.

With my friend Diane, I share my most joyous thanks for her unconditional love. This friend of more than twenty years nurtured me when I was but a broken-winged bird. Her love has never wavered, and we have shared and will share the joys of our ever-changing lives.

To my friend, Marilyn Innerfeld, who lives her life with an open and questing heart—we came back together in this lifetime so that you, through your experience of us, can come to know fully once again the you as God that you are. I can find no words to thank this friend, except to celebrate our lives, love and joy. I do so with my heart fully open and invite you to know that Marilyn works with love as a healer and teacher in every moment.

I am blessed to carry their love in my heart across time and forever.

A Thought

This is *your* experience.
I am but the messenger.

The Simple Truth...

CHAPTER 1

On Becoming
The Messenger

In October 1998, I heard a "voice" that changed my life. But it was August 1983 when I made the choice that awakened that voice.

Little did I know in 1998 that my life had prepared me for a singular path—to teach the world the Simple Truth that each of us is God. I now understand that it is no coincidence that I am the messenger of this Simple Truth. The story of my life, which I share in this chapter, will give you insight into how my life prepared me to write this book, what it means to live in selflove, and how I came to this very powerful moment as a messenger who lights the way.

The story that I share with you is my experience of life events that I had with my family and friends. I have come to understand that each of us experiences the shared moments of our lives differently because we are manifesting that experience in order to learn from our own hearts. Neither my parents nor friends would describe these moments the same way because they were choosing them to learn something else. This is my story.

In 1983, I was living in Boston, Massachusetts, and had just completed my bar exam to become a lawyer. I was also deeply depressed, and as I scribbled a suicide note and contemplated how I would end my life, I had no idea that I was about to make a powerful choice of selflove that would one day bring me to this moment.

From the age of twelve, I had become increasingly depressed. Three powerful factors contributed to this depression. While I had had a very loving and joy-filled life as a child, my heart was burdened by an experience of sexual abuse as a four-year old and by my choice to keep this experience a secret. This secret progressively ate away at me emotionally, while I searched for a safe person to speak to about it. It was not until my early twenties that I did so.

When I turned twelve, my family made the first of two moves during my teenage years, resulting in my struggling with loss of identity and loneliness. Each move required starting over, meeting all new friends and the loss of almost all former relationships. On my third move in six years, when I left for college, I could barely bring myself to put forth the effort to start over again.

In addition, my parents, who were loving and hardworking, believed that success in life was more assured if one had a professional degree. I grew up with a clear understanding that my career choices were one of four: doctor, dentist, lawyer or architect. My sister became a dentist, my brother an architect, and I became a lawyer. We all sought to please our parents but found it difficult to carve out our individual identities during our formative teenage years.

Throughout my teens, as I struggled with depression and watched my siblings manifest their pain in different ways, I asked my parents if we might go to counseling as a family. It was not something they could face, given the pain in their hearts from their own childhoods. It was not that they did not love us. It was that they did not understand that they could choose joy rather than pain and fear. We did not go to counseling. This was not a road we walked together.

When I was seventeen, I also made a powerful choice to leave the Catholic Church and cease being a practicing

Catholic. In my youth, I had found great peace in the structure of the church, but as I grew older, I no longer felt comfortable with my experience. At first, this choice left me feeling more adrift than ever, but it allowed me to recognize that I was a spiritual person, even if I did not practice an institutional religion. I committed myself to living the best life I could, in all moments.

Throughout my teenage and college years, I achieved in school as a top student, graduating Phi Beta Kappa from college and becoming a student leader and an athlete. Despite my achievements, I had to struggle to maintain balance and to find peace and joy. I buried myself in my academics and found ways to cope and continue to grow. Sports were my outlet, and my complete focus on tennis throughout my teens shifted to running in college.

Immediately after college, I chose to attend law school. As I neared the completion of law school, I found myself in the depths of my depression. While my depression was not undetected by those around me, none of them understood its depth. To know darkness everyday, and yet function, required all my heart could summon and almost all of my energy.

In some ways, death seemed like the only option. I had asked for help. I had tried what others had said would make me happy. I felt so alone. I also did not know how to go on, or if life would ever be different. I had come to believe that, if we had one moment of joy in our lives, then our lives were fulfilled.

But the morning I contemplated committing suicide, I suddenly recalled moments of pure joy from my childhood. I had experienced a wonderful childhood. My parents were loving and dedicated. All my needs were met. As a child, I had been allowed to fully experience freedom and joy. For my parents, parenting became more emotionally complicated when I reached my teenage years.

What changed my decision to commit suicide was a powerful childhood memory of jumping a fence and rolling in the grass. As I experienced that memory and the joy I recalled, I knew once again that joy existed. I realized that the problem was that, at that time, I just did not know such joy in my everyday life.

Rather than end my life due to the darkness of ten years of depression, I chose instead to find one moment of joy in each day and accept the rest as I experienced it. I also decided that, for the rest of my life, I would make every decision based on whether that choice gave me joy, no matter what anyone else believed was "right" for me. I chose to love myself and healed my heart as I did.

Within days of receiving word from the Massachusetts Bar that I had passed the bar exam, I called my family and told them I would not practice law. It was a shock to my parents, family and friends. While I could have practiced law, I knew that I would never have been "successful" if I was not in joy. Instead, I embarked upon a search for work that was joyous for me.

In the years to come, I had many challenging moments, both financially and personally. I had eight jobs in eleven years. I found joy in entrepreneurial environments. They were alive, creative and exciting. They were also financially volatile. Many times, I could feel the disbelief of my friends and family when I experienced another period of unemployment. Nevertheless, I never swayed from my commitment to follow my joy.

In those years, I began to learn what it was that brought me joy, and I gained great confidence about "selling" myself to employers. I could sit in an interview and explain what type of work I was good at and passionate about doing for them. My clarity helped me carve out positions built on both my strengths and my passion.

Those seventeen years were increasingly expansive and joyous. It took four years after choosing not to commit suicide for me to find myself living in light and happiness, rather than darkness and pain. During those four years, I worked with a psychologist, who guided me to acknowledge the experiences in my heart. She is gifted and I have been forever grateful to her for her work with me, and to my close friend, Diane, who told me to seek professional help.

I also opened my heart and followed it to meet my husband Ben. He came into my life a few years after my lowest moment, at a time when I was finally beginning to live in the light and feel joy in each day. He is an unusual man, loving and sensitive and committed to enjoying life. He taught me how to reawaken my sense of humor and to have fun. He had clarity about what was most important to him, which was and is family. We laughed and played as we shared the beginnings of a life together.

What I discovered was that my choice to find joy in each day, and to choose according to my own joy, led me into a life of freedom and fun. Life became lighter and lighter. Each year became more expansive. I grew in knowing who I am and loving myself. I recognized the courage of my choices. I loved my willingness to follow my own path, while watching others struggle because they were fearful of doing so. I felt alive as I explored the world and relished what I loved—art, sports, my body, my sexuality, my laughter and my leadership abilities.

In my twenties and thirties, I believed that there was some force greater than myself that guided life. I was open to spiritual truths and experiences but was not a seeker. Periodically, I had unusual or paranormal experiences, but I did not pursue them or judge them. I just found them fascinating.

Over time, I carved out a wonderful career in marketing, and in my early thirties began my own consulting company in partnership with a friend. We owned this company together for seven years and successfully worked with many prominent Fortune 500 companies. I loved building our business and working with bright, dedicated clients and co-workers.

Ben and I also had two children. They changed my life, because they taught me about unconditional love, joy and balance. I had always been a Type-A person. My drive covered my pain and fed my joy of learning. Parenting awakened my heart to make choices that would honor my children's needs for love and security— choices that also taught me to honor myself.

In October 1998, my life changed in a very extraordinary way. At that time, I was running my business, raising my family and sharing a wonderful life with my husband. During a visit to Colorado with a friend, we stayed with Marilyn and Hank Innerfeld. At that time, I did not know them personally, although I had been a client of theirs since they are both intuitives. While visiting them, I told Marilyn how, each night as I lay down to sleep, I watched a movie with characters who appeared in my third eye, the space in the middle of the forehead. She asked me if I had ever talked with them. It had never occurred to me to do so.

That night, as I closed my eyes, I said I wanted to speak with them. During the night I bolted awake, hearing the most beautiful and clear "voice" in my head, sharing the following message for Hank:

The firekeeper's role is to nurture and tend the fire. But the firekeeper must be patient, for the fire decides how it will grow. It is a waiting, watching and knowing role, for the fire has its own power. Honor that power with patience.

As I wrote down this message, I was moved by its beauty. In the morning, I shared it, believing that this voice had only spoken to me so that I could share something with Hank and Marilyn. Little did I know that, from that moment forward, any question I asked would be answered in beautiful, poetic language.

I spent the rest of that weekend joyously sharing this discovery with my friends. I also found myself experiencing a powerful connection with Marilyn, whom I had just come to meet. It was as if I had known her forever and was becoming reacquainted. We spent a day together at the Garden of the Gods in Colorado

Springs, a beautiful park with massive rock outcroppings, discovering a oneness of experience, friendship and love. I returned home to Virginia changed.

Back home, I shared my experience with my husband. He was surprised but accepting. I continued my work as a marketing consultant and mother, but spent many evenings, after I put my children to sleep, keeping a journal of messages on everything— love, creation, abundance, lack, hatred, pain and joy.

I found that my body changed. I needed only four hours of sleep, ate different foods, and life felt increasingly lighter and freer. Ben noticed that our family changed as I changed, and we experienced more joy and fun.

In late November, I began to receive messages about how my life had prepared me for a singular path. The messages spoke of my choices as a leader, my willingness to stand against the tide, and how I had experienced love. I understood about my life choices having prepared me, because many times I had chosen to be a leader, despite the consequences, and to live what I believed, rather than say one thing and do another. I had not known what I had been preparing to do.

In December, I received a message that said that everything would be taken care of for me, and that I should make time. I looked up from my chair in the basement office in our home and saw something quite unusual. It was a ticket line of souls—beings of all ages, races and nationalities. I heard that they had been waiting a long time to speak with me, and that I should make time to hear them.

I sat there for hours, writing down a description of each, their life stories and what they wanted to teach. I learned so much from each one and felt honored to hear their words. One of those on line was a young boy named Eric. He introduced himself as my son from another lifetime. I was in shock and cried. Before long, I would come to know him much better.

At this time, I was sharing my messages with only three people, because such experiences were not part of my life or my relationships with colleagues or friends. My work and family life were going on "normally," although many things were being experienced differently. Even my former business partner, a scientist by nature, noticed that I was more relaxed and peaceful, even though she did not know of my messaging.

Within a week, I heard that I had a singular life path to follow during this lifetime. I heard that it would not be easy, and maybe even quite difficult. I heard that I was a messenger of the Simple Truth that each of us is God. It was my life path to walk the Earth teaching this Truth.

I was shocked, because I was not a religious or spiritual person in any traditional sense. The next day, I walked in the woods to contemplate this choice and realized that we all have it backwards.

Fundamentally, many, if not most people on Earth, believe that God—the spirit or force of creation—is all-powerful and only of goodness, light and love. Many believe there is pain on the Earth because mankind, through choices and actions, has corrupted that which is divine, either within themselves or in all that has been created by God. But the truth is that we are God, and, as God, we choose pain or joy in order to learn that there is no separation between ourselves and God.

I realized that no one has taught us this Truth, and that, if we understand it, we can choose differently. We can choose joy.

In that moment, I understood that no one teaches us that pain is a choice. I knew that I was here to teach all people that they are magnificent, perfect, all-powerful and, as such, can choose joy. The world can change with this Truth. In that moment, I chose to walk my path.

Within days of that choice, I heard I was to write a book called *The Simple Truth About God*. I heard the chapter titles as well. A week later, in January 1999, I heard that it was time to write it. In seven nights, I wrote the book you are choosing to read. It was like transcribing, because I listened and typed the beautiful words shared by the "voice" I heard—which I now understand is the voice of my heart.

I considered myself the first listener and was honored to be so. It is a beautiful book of Truth. The hearts of many across time reached out in eloquent and challenging words, so that you, too, could awaken to this Simple Truth. I learn from it everyday in the process of sharing it with the world.

I have made only grammatical changes to the original text of this book. It uses the language of the heart, which is one that, for many readers, sounds stilted or odd. I understand now that it sounds that way because we are accustomed to a language filled with judgment, pain and separation. It is odd how the language and sounds of our hearts are so unknown to us.

A week after completing *The Simple Truth About God*, I was asked by Eric to write a second book, entitled *Heart Songs: Messages for Parents from Children Across Time*. I made time to do so at night and wrote this book in two weeks. It is a beautiful book about unconditional love.

Within weeks of choosing to walk my path, I had two manuscripts. Since I had chosen to walk the Earth, teaching all who choose to listen that each of us is God, I began to walk around my neighborhood, sharing the manuscripts. I was met with shock, fear and some curiosity.

I also reached out to my parents and siblings to share the story of my experience and these books. My family reacted with shock and great fear. Ben experienced challenging comments from those who were trying to understand what was happening. My parents asked me to see a doctor. I told them I could understand that they might think I was ill, but that I knew I was well. I had known great mental illness and conflict in the past. However, I knew I was well and experiencing joy. I thanked them for their love and did not choose to see a doctor. They have since watched me as I embarked upon a new life and come to accept me. The underlying truth is that they always loved me.

I embarked upon a changed life. To live this life as a messenger of this powerful Truth, I understood that I had to be willing to let go of everything I had ever experienced. I had to let go of my self-perception, reputation, humility, career, and maybe even my children. I knew that many people would be afraid of me or very uncomfortable. Others would question why I was this messenger and teacher, when they were the ones who had spent time studying spiritual truth. I knew that some would think I was the anti-Christ or devil. I knew that I would often stand alone as I shared this Truth with many who are in great fear.

I also knew that, if at any time my husband should be overwhelmed by this experience, he would have plenty of evidence to use in a court of law, in order to gain custody of our children. But I chose to continue on my path, even if it were to mean that I would not be with my children as often until they reached adulthood. There would be no more powerful lesson I could teach them than to live their own paths and follow their hearts. The night I experienced this powerful choice to let go of my children, I wept.

During the following months, my life changed in profound ways. I discovered that I had the gift of medical intuition, was gifted to do energetic healing work with children, could work with the essence or soul of a person and could powerfully teach what it means to live as God. In June 1999, I chose to sell my business to my partner. I walked away from our success, although this was quite difficult, since building a business is like raising a child. But I could not honor my partner or our clients while living an increasingly dual life, working as a consultant during the day and doing healing and teaching work with clients at night.

In July 1999, I moved with my family to Colorado. In October, I co-founded *The Worldwide Center* with my friend Marilyn Innerfeld. The change for our family felt magical, and our lives unfolded at breakneck speed in an experience of joy we could never have imagined.

Everything resulted from the choice to live and share the Simple Truth that each of us is God. When asked who I am or what I do, I never falter. I always share my story and purpose. Ben and I chose to let go and follow our joy, knowing that all our experiences would reflect the choice we had made to love ourselves.

During the years since this moment of great change, I have worked one-on-one with many individuals who are seeking to experience joy, peace, and personal fulfillment. I have been challenged with many questions about what it means to live as God. In 2001, I wrote the final chapter entitled "The Understanding" to *The Simple Truth About God*, in order to answer the most commonly asked questions and to help readers understand what it means to be God.

I also came to understand that my life choices for the seventeen years prior to 1998 had been about living in selflove. I had experienced all that I am now teaching, without ever understanding it as selflove. My life had prepared me to be a messenger of *The Simple Truth About God*. I know that everyone on Earth is equal as God. While we are the same, our understanding of this Truth is different. I am here to light the way because I, like no other, understand.

I chose to walk this path. I choose it everyday, in every moment, by how I choose to live. It is a path like all others. It is about experiencing oneself as All.

Now, I live in joy-beyond-joy. At times, I cannot find the words to help people understand what this feels like. I have few experiences that are not peaceful, joy-filled and magical. I am honored by all who choose to love themselves and to reach out to understand what that means.

The Simple Truth About God is a gift of my heart. It powerfully shares the message that each of us is God. If you choose to live this Truth, your life will be changed completely. You will be empowered with both an understanding of the source of your power and with the tools to live every moment fully and joyfully.

All will change the instant that you love yourself as perfect. Know that every moment is of great purpose, and choose to learn in joy-beyond-joy.

I share this and All that I am with an open heart.

CHAPTER 2

The Simple Truth...
About God

You Are God.

God is One, God is All, YOU are God.

For so many, this Simple Truth has been taken away, stolen in the night of your life with little notice. Yet, there is nothing more important to one's lifetime and lifetimes than understanding and knowing this Simple Truth.

While you have been taught that God is glorious, pure and perfect, you have also been taught that you can never be God. Everything that is you was stolen in the moment when you experienced that lesson as truth. For most, that moment occurred long before you were five years old. Like a tidal wave, the world around you told you to look in awe outside yourself at the glory and beauty that is our world and give thanks to everyone but yourself.

Could your life on Earth be so insignificant as to be only that of a spectator? Could all be spectators except for one that no one has ever seen? Could one deserve all the gratitude and all others ingratitude? Why does this make sense to you when, in your private life, and in your most private moments, you experience the incredible gift that you are to this world and to those in your life? Yet, most remain quiet, afraid to dare even to suggest that those moments are, in their essence, the pure experience of the love that you are—God-within.

God-within, not God-without. God-within is a celebration of self, a love from a fully open heart that accepts without question the glory of who you are and why you are here in every moment you experience as your life. God-within does not judge anything, including, and most importantly, oneself. God is love—selflove. Love is acceptance.

God-without does not exist. God-without is your creation, fully empowered by your thoughts and beliefs. God as vengeful is only the experience of your own self-hate and self-punishment. God as forgiving is only the experience of your desire for selflove. God-without, as all-powerful, is only the experience of your darkness.

But God-within *is* all-powerful and *is* the Creator of all, just as you are taught about God-without. For many people, that is quite a scary and overwhelming thought. For, as God, you are all-powerful, the creator of all that is your world, our world and the Universe.

Yes, you *are* accountable for being you and for choosing the you that you are and the we, as you, that you become. It appears so much easier to think that someone else is responsible for your life, your health, your opportunities, your challenges, your choices, your happiness and your joy. It is actually harder, because you must continually diminish yourself to empower the Other.

Know that, throughout time and at the birth that you experienced this lifetime, you fully knew that you are God—God-within. While you were without words, you were not without the fire of your soul's purpose. It was lit like a bonfire. Recall how, in childhood moments, those around you began to convince you to be less than the one that you are—parents diminished your dreams and visions; teachers grouped you by expectations; neighbors compared you to siblings and friends. Soon you held back. Soon you forgot.

For most, sadly, it is only at the moment of their death that they remember. But in that moment, as they learn their deepest life lesson, they fully regain this knowledge and the experience that this knowledge provides. Whether it is a child who dies in the crib, a teenage girl who overdoses on drugs, or a frail, old woman who dies comfortably in her sleep, the poignancy of that moment is never lost. In death, this knowledge is reawakened, the bonfire re-lit and fueled with a celebration of self as God.

But it does not have to be this way. There is another way.

Over a three-month period, in this lifetime that I am now experiencing, I was honored to be visited by many who, in the moment of death, reawakened the knowledge of God-within. They, too, in the poignancy of that moment of death, awakened an urgency to share with others who were left behind this all-important lesson. Throughout this book of Simple Truth, I will share their stories and lessons so that, as they desire, they can reach you in this lifetime that you experience as now.

Know that, for them, this sharing is a release for their souls. It allows them to be part of the creation that we all are of one another and to continue to be so.

There is only one way to teach you about God, for God is All. While every visitor who will share a story throughout this book is God, there is only one way to learn about God—as you read this book, become the God you are. This book will challenge you to question all your long-held beliefs and to move, even if for only a moment, to the place that is you as the God that you are. To prepare you, God-As-All shares with you this message:

Dear One, this book is written in the voice and words of God. You <u>are</u> loved. You have always, in every moment, been loved unconditionally by many and by God-As-All. You are of the living energy that is God in All, and every moment of your life either appreciates it or diminishes its power through neglect.

Dear One, you are only asked to do one thing as the living energy of God—celebrate you! Celebrate! Celebrate! Celebrate! Dance in the streets and sing from the mountaintops that you are you! Tell the world that you are wonderful and glorious, just as you are.

When was the last time you said, "I *love* me?" When was the last time you thanked yourself for being you, the gift that you are to all others? Have you *ever* done that? Dear One, there is nothing else to do but celebrate you and your magnificence. NOTHING.

But you protest, how could this be so? How could we all be God? Why are there so many religions and so many who believe in so many gods? Because, through all time, man has seen himself through his mind and not his heart. For, as God, man sees with his heart. As man, man feels with his heart and lives with his mind.

But the mind, Dear One, is so much more limited than the heart. Ask yourself how love would be if it were merely a "decision" that one made like a shopping decision. It would be empty and devoid of joy. Yet man has exalted the mind and ignored the heart. Intellect over Knowing.

With his mind, man has decreed that glory is external and, if embraced, can be felt fleetingly, internally. Man has created obstacles and challenges to spiritual reunion with the essence of God. Man has created images, rituals, requirements, punishments and limits, all with his mind. Man has built monuments and houses of worship as calling places for those who seek that which is inside them. Man has sought comfort in numbers.

You ask how they could all be wrong. Because they all are. Because so few, through all time, have been willing to stand against the tide of so many and share the Truth. Imagine yourself standing as the only one telling all listeners that what they believe is so much less than what is. Imagine telling them that the god and gods they have exalted, built kingdoms for and of, are mere creations of the externalized energy that they are. Imagine, throughout history, what happened to those who did so. Do you understand now why so few who know this Truth have shared it?

Imagine again, though, a world in which you know this Truth to be so, and all others know this Truth to be so. Would it not also be difficult for one to stand against _that_ tide? It is not a tide; it is a tidal wave. So, as God-as-All, you are being asked only, if but for the moments while you read this book, to experience, in privacy, yourself as God—God-within. For then, many of you will awaken or *begin to awaken to the Truth that God is One, God is All, You are God.*

Dear One, to awaken you I will guide you with all the energy of God-within to the experience of God-within. Go to your heart, Dear One, by thinking deeply about someone you love unconditionally. Someone you would give your life for at a moment's notice. Feel that love fully. Let it encompass you and become you. Stay in that love.

Now, think about someone whom you believe loves you unconditionally —your parents, a close friend, a spouse or a child. If you have no one, think about the god that you believe is outside yourself. Let that same unconditional love wash over you, until it feels as it did moments ago when you thought of someone you love. This may take some time, because you may find it harder to allow yourself to believe that someone loves you unconditionally.

When those energies are the same, say, "I love God. I am God. I love Me," one hundred times. Stay in that energy while you do this. When you are done, thank yourself for being the you that you are.

Now you are ready to understand how to live as you as God-within. Celebrate yourself everyday and encourage all others, especially children, to do so. For every time you celebrate yourself, your words and energies fuel the fire that is you—your soul purpose and essence.

Live! God is of life! While you have been told to "contemplate" your god, Dear One, "celebrate" you as God instead. Find what speaks to your heart and make the choices you need to in order to _live_ that passion. And, Dear One, live it! Know that there are no bounds, no limits and no obstacles to your doing so. Be who you are and let others be who they are. Stop creating obstacles and rules. Stop saying, "I can't do that because...." Know that, as you, you are totally loved and will live in the abundance of you as God-within.

Does this mean you will feel no pain, suffer no barbs and sail through life? No. To live means to experience your life. It means to know that life is full of lessons that call forth deeper understandings about the power of being God-within. Each of these understandings should be celebrated, for they are of you, created by you, for you.

It means you have choices, though. Choose how you will live, because as God-within, you can choose how you

The Simple Truth...

will experience what you choose. Know that all that you experience is your choice and your creation.

Spend a moment, Dear One, and think about your life. How much joy do you experience everyday? Do you wake up excited about your day? Do you feel loved by family and friends? Do you spend your days doing something that excites you and gives you joy? Do you experience illness? Are you happy? Do you tell those you love that you love them, spontaneously and often? Is your life fantastic?

Pretend to take a paintbrush in your hand and paint a picture of your life as the greatest vision that you could have of it. Who loves you? How do you live? What do you do each day? Are you married? Do you have children? How much do you dance and play? What do you know? How happy are you? How healthy are you? How fantastic does your life feel? Take time with this painting, for the more detailed you are, the more your life will begin to look like your picture. Hang it in your heart and visit it every day. Honor it with the knowledge that, if you think it as the God-within that you are, it will be.

"How could this be?" you say. "This is absurd." Why is this any more absurd then thinking that there is a big

Santa in the sky, who gives and takes everything away from you, depending upon how you act? Now, that is absurd! Why do you find it so easy to disempower yourself? Why is it so hard to know and trust that, as a responsible being, you will make responsible and honorable choices that are right for you? Given the choice, would you let someone steal your heart? Then why do you let them steal your soul, the essence of you?

Understand, though, as best you can, that as God-within, you are pure love. Love is pain. Love is joy. Love is acceptance. Selflove as God-within is acceptance unconditionally of self. If you fill yourself with doubt, if you allow yourself to feel fear, if you focus on what you "think" are weaknesses, then you will become less than what you are. Then you will diminish the power that is you, for you are God.

Now, Dear One, be cautioned. There is a difference between I AM GOD and I am God. You are God, but know that God is ALL. Everyone you meet is God, just as you are. For together, as you call upon this knowledge, you create your world.

I hear the questions of your children and yourselves: "Even the bad guys?" "What about the dictators, the robbers, the abusers and cruel leaders?" Yes, <u>they</u> are God, too. But they made and are making life choices that are not about celebrating themselves, but about self-hatred. That self-hatred ultimately robs the soul of its joy. At some point, the soul can no longer feel joy and it dies. These choices are no less valid, though. As lessons and learning, they are just as valid as honorable choices that enrich the soul.

"What of those hurt by the life choices of others?" you ask. Yes, you created Hitler, for you are Hitler. Hitler was an individual demonized by his own self-hate, created by the energy of those who most fear one like Hitler. For in the instant that you allow yourselves to conceive of someone or something so powerful that it could rob you of your soul, you create the energy that can become that demon. Think it and it will be.

Know that you all have created such energies throughout your lifetimes. In every moment of this lifetime when you do not love yourself as the God that you are, you invite yourself to be less. You, too, are capable of being

Hitler, for you are but the choices that you make about how you celebrate yourself. Choose wisely from your heart.

I have one more lesson for you, Dear One—see the world through God's eyes. Look at the magnificence that you are and that your world is. Stop to watch a flower unfold in the sunshine, marvel at sunrise and sunset, listen to the streams and rivers sing, honor the beauty of the Earth, appreciate the abundance that you are and have, embrace your life, and know that there are no obstacles.

Through God's eyes, you will see the glory that is you. Wake up each day in appreciation and thanks to yourself. Live each day in celebration of self. Experience each day as the moment that it is—your first and last. Rejoice, Exalt, Be, for this is the Simple Truth about God—God is One, God is All, You are God.

You have many questions, I know. All can and will be answered. Ask them and listen for the answers, for they will be there for you in your world. In the chapters that follow, Dear One, you will learn answers to many of the questions that mankind allows to separate itself from itself—God-within. Messengers like you, who lived lifetimes without an understanding of God-within, will share their deepest lessons about joy and pain, love and hate, abundance and lack, life and death, and choice. Each one is like you—average and magnificent, hopeful and fearful, covetous and envious. Each one, like you, is on a journey across lifetimes to learn the Simple Truth. They come to you, so that you may learn from them and them from you.

You are the miracle. You are God. Rejoice! Exalt! Be! For God-As-All rejoices in you!

CHAPTER 3

The Simple Truth...
About Joy and Pain

Joy is of You! Pain is of You! Choose how you want to be.

Let us speak first of joy. Joy is of you on the inside. It has no bounds and no limits, for it is the distance between the farthest reaches of your imagination and your inner grounding—your soul. It has nothing to do with what things you have, those around you, your goals or what others think of you. It is your experience of you.

How much joy can you possibly imagine? Imagine it, and it will be there.

You have been taught and told that joy is derived from and through something, but joy simply is. It need not be earned and needs no permission. To find the joy that you are, do not focus on the outside; go inside. Spend time with you in your world. Celebrate you, and you will experience the joy that you are.

If you do not, you will ultimately create pain. For pain is a choice. It is created, empowered and owned by you. It is a reflection of the diminished soul, for without selflove, the soul energy withers like a flower without water. Pain can be experienced as illness, sadness, mental anguish, stress, anger, remorse or cruelty. You have total control over it, for you are its creator.

Weaken its bonds by loving yourself with the conviction of the Truth that you are God-within. If you do not, pain ultimately begets death, often a physical death that is premature. Love yourself to the fullest life you can imagine.

A ten-year-old boy named Amman

I live in a desert. The winds are hot and the air dry. I come to you, for you are sharing a lesson about the most important experience of life—joy of self. It matters not that we often do not have enough water and our throats are parched. It matters not that the sand from the wind pelts our skin and burns. We are a happy and joyous people, for we live inside ourselves. We see ourselves through our eyes as God and know that we are God. We are perfect as we are.

Joy is the energy created by the soul that loves itself. The soul is a living energy that is fueled like a fire by its own love. I ask not what I do not have. I look not outside at the desert. I seek not the judgments of others. I feel only the love in my heart for myself.

What do you want to teach?

I want to teach others that no one can give them joy. Even the joy of watching a child is but the experience of self as a child—unlimited by thought, expectation and rules. Joy is the heat from the fire, and it is dampened every time one allows oneself to compare and seek happiness outside.

Tell them to go inside. Tell them to imagine the greatest amount of joy that they could withstand, and then let that joy be. For it will be. Thank them for listening.

A three-year-old boy with blond hair, named Allen

Hey! I am ALLEN THE GREAT! I love myself a lot. Do you know why?

Why?

Because I am me. You know, before I died and came here, I was really loved. Every day, my mom and dad told me that they loved me. And every time I heard that, my heart jumped in joy. My dad used to call me "Allen the Great," and I am. He was right. I miss my dad and my mom, and I will always miss hearing them say, "I love you." But you know what? Until I came here, I did not understand how important it was that I said, "I love me" every day. For once I started saying that, then my heart really started jumping. Now I'm just jumping for joy all the time. Tell them to let their hearts jump for joy, too. I gotta go. Thanks.

---◆---

A very old woman, who is hunched over

---◆---

What is your name?

My name is not important. My story is. I was beaten as a child, raped as a wife, discarded by my husband. But I lived a long life with joy in my heart. How could that be, you say? It is and was, because no one can take your joy but you. Believe me, they will try. From their joyless place, they seek to take yours. Know that it is protected and, even in the most difficult moments, all is of your creation and perception.

If you see pain for yourself, you will feel pain, for you have seen the opposite of joy. Pain is a creation of a self that looks outside for validation and love. Pain is a self that looks with eyes of unworthiness and thereby begets that experience.

Pain is created; joy is experienced. For, at your birth, you are, in your totality, infinitely in a place of joy. You are with you and in celebration of you. There are no limits for you, so experience none.

What do you most want to teach?

Teach them to love themselves inside. Tell them that, if they love themselves, their joy will grow. Tell them there are no limits. Be who they are in all of their magnificence, and they will experience the full joy of who they are—God-within. Thank you.

---◆---

A middle-aged man named Daniel

---◆---

I am Daniel. I was a farmer, a father, a husband and a church-going man. I believed God was all-powerful and granted joy and happiness to other God-fearing folks. But now I know differently. I spent my life praying for happiness, for my life was about work, duty and responsibility. I had a good life and, at most times, felt happy or, at least, pleased with what I had.

What do you want to teach us?

I missed out on everything. Life is about living, not serving. Life is about being all that your heart seeks to be, not all that you believe others want you to be. I always thought having a family and farm was the good life. Now, having experienced the God that I am, I understand what you need to know. It is not about the good life; it is about the great life. Good is settling for so little.

Joy and happiness are experienced by so few, for most buy into the rules and roles dictated by others. You actually find pleasure in sharing your misery and feel embarrassed to share your joy. Isn't that strange? Watch children. They always share joy. Why do you teach them to share pain and hide joy? Steal not their openness to be the joy that they are by asking them questions about how they could be better or telling them they are not good enough. Who are you really speaking to, anyway?

Tell them they do not have to miss out. Choose to be the joy that they are. Live their life, not the life others see for them. It is all up to them. Thank you for sharing this. We love you all.

A young girl of four named Mary

I died a painful death and lived a short, but painful life. I was born all wrong—my limbs were wrong, my body looked wrong, and my mind was not right. All I remember are people saying how sorry they were and how bad they felt. Every time I heard that, my world got darker and I felt more pain.

Do you know that, only late at night, as my mother would cry in my room, did I hear her whisper that she loved me? It was hard to love me, I guess. Everyone felt that she had done something wrong, so it was hard for her to love herself, let alone me. Finally, all the pity and the lack of love created so much pain that I died. Why couldn't they love me so that I could love myself?

What do you want to teach them?

Tell them that they create their own pain. Tell them to believe me, for inside each of them is a place that understands total selflove—God-within. And each and every day that they do not love themselves, they create and embrace the energy of pain. Tell them to tell others to share love with them, for through the feeling of love—true unconditional love—they can begin to learn to love themselves. When they do, they will begin to experience joy and no longer experience pain. Choose joy; it is so much better. Thank you for loving them enough to do this.

—✦—

An older man in a rocking chair, Who is very much at peace

—✦—

You know what? They think that joy is an emotion. They are wrong. Tell them it is a way of being. It is the experience of themselves as the beings that they are in the farthest reaches of their imaginations, grounded in their inner souls. Now, that's a mouthful. It just means that it is who they are, not what they can feel because of others and the Other.

If joy were an emotion, it would come from someplace or something. It is of the "between." Tell them to see themselves as all they would hope to be and then feel themselves as that vision. Everyday they must see this vision again and again, so that soon it becomes the only vision that they see and the only way they know to feel themselves. Tell them to do this everyday. Thanks.

─◆─
God-As-All
─◆─

What is the difference between joy and happiness?

Happiness is contentment; joy is ecstasy. Most of you have never experienced joy, except in moments of sexual union. At least, many of you have allowed yourself those moments.

Why does this matter?

It matters because, if you cannot experience joy, you cannot experience the love of others, abundance and perfection. It matters because life is about living, and so few of you are doing so. Rejoice! Exalt! Be!

The Simple Truth...

CHAPTER 4

The Simple Truth...
About Love and Hate

Love is not an emotion. Love is the passion inside you that celebrates the self. Selflove begets all love. No one can give you the experience of love except yourself, for without selflove, everything that you experience in your life as love is but a whisper in the wind.

Selflove is totally unconditional. You have no faults, no weaknesses and no blemishes. You, as you are, are in your perfection, for, in your perfection, you are the God-within that you are.

Around you, you have built a world focused on becoming something or someone else. You read about others' lives and dream about what it would be like to be them; you let others dictate how you dress; you let others tell you what you need to "improve." You focus so much energy on your bodies. You focus on everything but that which is most important to everything else—you as you are in your perfection.

Loving yourself is easy, compared to neglecting and even hating yourself as you do. It takes so much more energy to be and become something that you are not.

Have you ever stepped back to consider that everyone on the Earth is uniquely here, as they are, for a purpose? Everyone. Why, then, would you want to be like anyone else? Why, then, would you not take great pride and joy in who you are and why you are uniquely here? No one else is here with the same purpose and profile. No one!

Why not focus your energy on enjoying your life? Every aspect of it is here so that you can learn and grow. *Every* aspect. If you have experienced pain, loss, love or hate, all are of your creation. Imagine spending time being with yourself and spending more time creating a life rich in ever greater learning. To do that, begin by loving yourself everyday for who you uniquely are on Earth! Love your life, too.

As you let go of your neglect and self-hate, you will discover that you were robbing yourself of the full experience of who you are in life. You will re-ignite the fire of selflove inside. For, over time, as you look outside yourself with desire, envy and self-recrimination, the fire that was yours at birth lessens and, for some, is extinguished. There is no time for delay. Say, "I love me, I love me, and I love me," with conviction and feeling. Say it! Mean it! Be it!

Know that God is pure love. Know that *you* are pure love. Feel the love that you are. Let it overwhelm you and watch how your world will change.

However, one cannot speak of love on the Earth without talking about relationships. So many of you yearn for relationships of deep and meaningful love. But you have it all backwards. You seek to merge yourself in the other. What are you doing?

Relationships are about two souls, each celebrating itself, entering into a union of joy, for each, in celebrating itself, celebrates the other. Understand that you will find or strengthen a relationship when you love yourself enough that the fire inside you, as a joyous energy, attracts another. It is about self, not other.

Know that love is an expression of the inner passion you feel in your heart for yourself and your life journey. You will know you have all when you love yourself as the all that you are. Know that you are loved unconditionally by many. Know it, and then, *be* it.

⟶◇⟵

A young girl, five years old, with strawberry blond hair in braids. She is incredibly joyous in spirit

⟶◇⟵

Hi! I am so happy to be talking with you. I miss my mom, but I have a secret to tell you.

What?

I am God and I am love.

Why is that a secret?

No one says those things where you are. I thought it must be a secret. Isn't it? No one told me that when I was there. My mommy loved me, but I never loved myself, and I never thought I was God. Guess what?

What?

I have another secret for you.

What?

You are God and so are they. Guess what else? We each have a fire inside us that creates the most beautiful light. You should see how much light there is here. It is amazing. Anyway, can you tell my mom she's God and to love herself? She'd be a lot happier.

How will I know who she is?

She's very pretty, but, actually, tell everyone and she will hear, too. Thanks.

―◇―

A Native American elder—a chief

―◇―

You do not know love. I am an ancient chief and we have watched your people for lifetimes. You know hate and anger more than love, for you spend all your days searching for a you that you are not. We spent all our days celebrating the one that we were. We did not love the other as all, for to do so is to lessen the love, not strengthen it. We loved all that we are as One, all of the time, in everything.

Why do you find it so hard to be with yourself in love and joy? You are of the Earth and the Earth is magnificent. How can you marvel at the Earth's beauty and not marvel at your own? You are sunrise and sunset. You are the lake that reflects the fall leaves. You are the grandeur of the mountains and trickle of the streams. You are the sun inside.

You and your people look to us and think our respect for Mother Earth and Father Sky is to be respected. You miss the point. It is our respect for all as ourself that is most important. But you cannot see that, for you will not allow yourself. You want to be those aspects of us that you respect; but know that, unless you will respect and love yourself as All, then you will never love Mother Earth and Father Sky.

I have much to share with you, for I have witnessed lifetimes. But, most importantly, I must tell you about hate. All hate derives from self-hate. All. Hate is not a response to another. It is of one, inflicted on another and oneself. Your people hated us for being on lands they coveted. But we knew and know that the hate you felt was for the self that could not recognize its abundance with All.

Know that you and we are the Creators of the world. Love yourselves so that we can all love Mother Earth and Father Sky as the one that we are. Thank you for honoring me by listening.

---❖---

A very old woman with white hair

---❖---

I am Marcella. I was admired in my youth and lived the life of a princess. I was waited on, served and coiffed every day. All told me of my beauty with their words and eyes. I listened, but I did not hear, for when I looked in the mirror, I saw my imperfection. I saw my hair as limp and at times ugly. I saw my skin without polish and constant care. I saw the real shape of my body in its nakedness. I did not see beauty. I felt shame and imperfection.

I often wondered how they could not see. I tried to convince myself that they were right. I hid behind their words as a shield from the truth I thought they would realize one day. Even my loving husband, Prince Eric, never wavered in admiring my beauty. I thought, too, he was deceived. I waited and waited to be found out.

Guess what? Nothing happened. I got older and felt greater shame, but they still told me of my beauty. I died feeling shame. Now I mourn the waste of my life, for I see my beauty. I am beautiful! My beauty was striking and unique.

What do you want to teach them?

Teach them to love themselves. I could not or would not allow myself to love myself. I was afraid to feel and celebrate the me that I am. Tell them to look in the mirror with the eyes of God-within. For God sees magnificence! God sees perfection. See your perfection and experience it. Stop working on some "thing" you think you need to "change," to be beautiful and perfect. You are! Thank you for listening. I love the you that you are.

---◇---

Blackened souls of the Holocaust, many, many, many millions of them

---◇---

Dear Friends, we are the blackened souls of the Holocaust. Blackened by the hate that we created and died of. Strange how you all focus so much anger on those you think killed us. We killed ourselves. Do you not recognize that those that lived, lived because they loved themselves enough to create the energy of a sustained life? Many, like us, in the camps of hell, gave up on ourselves first, for we reacted in anger and hate. The camps were actually full of the same life that you experience when you go inside yourself. It is of the life essence. But the life essence is strangled and diminished by anger and hate.

What do you most want to teach us?

Love... Love...Love....

Love yourself, so you can love those you now hate, for in hating them, you really hate you. All are less.

You may not understand this, for you have been taught that both hate and love are of the other. Strange how you so easily believe that all is of the other. Can you not see how easy it was for us, the Jews and others of the camps, to create the energy of Hitler? Can you not see that you can and will do it again, unless you let yourself love yourself? We __are__ the blackened souls of the Holocaust. __Hear__ our cry. Love... Love...Love.

__Hear__ our cry. Love...Love...Love.

CHAPTER 5

The Simple Truth...
About Abundance and Lack

You have everything you ever need or want inside of you. You can call forth all that you need or want through who you are. You are God—the God-within.

You have no idea how much is available to you. How much do you not experience because you do not feel worthy to experience it? Why do you feel unworthy? You are God—the God-within. Why are you any less worthy than one you know who has called forth the experience you want? Will experiencing that which you want change you in some way that you are afraid of? Will being worthy change you in the eyes of those who know you, and in your own eyes? Are you more comfortable being unworthy?

What are you afraid will happen if you acknowledge that you are worthy of everything and anything that you can imagine and desire? Does saying that sound arrogant or selfish? Why are you comparing yourself to others and concerning yourself with what they will think? Think not of the other, think only of you. For the other, too, can also have all that they can imagine and desire. There is abundance for all.

What of those who have less? You ask, "Why, if we are God or there even is a god energy, do we have poverty and lack throughout the Earth?" We choose to. We create our lives and the world we live in with our thoughts. Do you not recognize that the focus of your philanthropic efforts on providing for unmet needs creates more unmet needs? Why not teach the starving how to love themselves and call forth the nourishing energy of All. From within themselves, they can sustain life while they learn to create life. Instead of spending your money, spend your time on teaching the lessons of God-within.

Know, too, that the rich man who yearns for more, yet is surrounded by the "things" brought by monetary wealth, and the starving man without food or comfort, are both lacking, for neither recognizes the abundance within. No soul lacks for anything. Those who perceive lack create it.

You choose, for you have everything inside of you. Look at your life and know that it is of your choosing. Love yourself as the God-within that you are, and you will find an abundance that will overwhelm you. Know that you will never lack for anything, as long as you know that as Truth.

---◈---

A young boy of two or three named Billy

---◈---

Hi! Thanks for talking with me. I'm Billy. My parents had everything except time for themselves to be themselves. They never had time to play and be. Funny, they spent so much time acquiring the things they thought would give them time that time went by. I played on my own with myself alot. It was kind of lonely.

What do you want to teach others?

I want you to tell them that the most important thing is to just be with themselves and love themselves. You know, it takes so little time to love oneself. It is a simple choice that reaps the greatest rewards one can imagine, for from that love one discovers oneself and what is really important. You know, my parents' "things" weren't really that important. They gave away that which was important for that which was not. Make a different choice—love yourself as the God-within and you will come to have all that you need, that which is important. Thanks. Tell my mom and dad I said hi!

---◇---

A middle-aged Indian man, who is emaciated

---◇---

I am Emow. I am hungry and I am full. To you, through your eyes of pity, I see your difficulty with my bony body. But you see only my skin and bones. Look into my eyes, and you will see into my soul. I am full. I know that my body is just a suit of clothes I wear, so that my soul can journey through this lifetime. My hunger is but one of the lessons I chose, so that I can better understand how to be the God-within that I am. I am like you. I do not yet understand how to be the God-within. But unlike you, I understand that this lifetime is of my choice and, at any moment, I can choose to be otherwise. I need only to change the knowing I have of my Truth. Pity me not, for it is not I that should be pitied, for I am full.

An upper-middle-class woman in her middle fifties, with white hair

You know, I always thought that if I just had that one more thing—a better car, a membership at the right club, the money to travel, more money in savings—then I would be happy, successful, and feel like I made it. Damn! More never mattered. I actually felt like I had less, the more I had. I had nothing, because I did not have me. You know what? I had more when I could get it, because I thought I would become more. The more I had, the more I stayed the same and even became less.

What do you want to teach others?

None of it matters, unless it matters to your heart as you. Do not think that to be spiritual is to be without, for that is crazy. To be spiritual is to be with all that is important to you and the you that is living your life. But nothing will "fill" the void that is love of self. Love of self will fill everything, for it calls forth the abundance. You are worthy. Love yourself! Love yourself, and in that love, call forth all that you will ever need or can imagine into your life. Tell them. Tell them for me.

A little, newborn baby

They call me baby. Their baby. You are wondering how I can teach you about abundance and lack. I am laughing, because you believe only those who "earn" abundance through the "work" of living a good life get abundance. That is so funny. It has nothing to do with worthiness. Nothing. We are all worthy. So, if all are worthy, how could it have to do with earning it? Do you ever wonder why the scoundrel wins out and takes the prize sometimes? You do, because you feel "cheated" when he does. Hey, give it up. The scam is on you. Stop trying to earn what you already have; everything you could ever need is inside. No one can give that to you but you. You just never do.

Strange, but I have more than most of you, because I realize that I have everything. What I do with my life will be of my choice and creation. It is a painting to behold and cherish, for it is mine. I realize that I do not have to do anything for anyone else in order to have what I need and want. I have what I need and want in order to do everything I want to do for myself in this lifetime. Now, that is fantastic!

The Simple Truth...

CHAPTER 6

The Simple Truth...
About Life and Death

Life is a mystery grander than the imagination. It is a gift to be cherished and filled with joy.

Life is not finite; it is a minuscule expression of the infinite. The only thing that is finite about life is our perception of it. Change your perception and you will experience yourself across time and through lifetimes of learning and growth. Know that you are the Creator of your life in this lifetime which you experience as now. Every thought, every decision and every act creates the experience that you choose. You are all-powerful, and you either realize it and live purposefully, or ignore it and live aimlessly.

You are here with a soul purpose, because across lifetimes you have lived, learning and growing in your understanding of the God-within. The soul is the living energy that is you. It does not know information about you; it is the experience of the you that you have created as God-within. It is a living experience. It is born of and with you, so that, in each lifetime that you experience, you carry the energy to fulfill with purpose the experience that will most aid you in growing to be one with the God-within—God-As-All.

Do not neglect the importance of this living energy, for it must be nurtured and appreciated to grow to be all that it can be. Take time each day to say to your soul, "Thank you for this wondrous journey that carries me across lifetimes in great joy." Appreciate your soul as much as you can, for when you do not, its fire dwindles and can be extinguished. Start now!

Know that whatever you think in life will be. When you focus your thoughts on illness, in fear, about lack, or in anger or hate, you create a life filled with that which you think of. Thoughts are all-powerful in life. Think, instead, about you and your unique gifts to the world and your world of friends and family, for all are gifts. Most just never realize it.

You will die as you presently perceive yourself. Death for you is the death of the physical body you wear. Know that death is so much more. It is merely a momentary shift across veiled worlds that offer opportunities for the soul to learn. Many live lives crossing between these worlds, with deaths they never realize or understand. You focus on one small moment, when you must focus on the moment that is your life for all time, across time. When you begin to focus on that moment, you will begin to live this lifetime you perceive as now.

Live each moment you perceive as if it is your first and last. In doing so, you will focus on living, not dying. Experience the fullness of the moment you are living by making choices that are of your heart and not your mind. Most, if not all, have yet to begin living. Think of your greatest moment of joy in the lifetime you are experiencing now. Know that all moments you experience can be so, if you choose them to be.

When your physical death occurs in this lifetime that you perceive as now, know that you will never be alone, except in judgment of your soul experience of this lifetime. There is no punishment awaiting you, for, as God-within, you are only accountable to yourself. Funny, how much time you waste in your world, focusing on what others will think or say, when all that matters is what *you* think or say.

Live *your* life! Let others live theirs!

Life is a mystery grander than one can imagine...

─◆─
A young boy of six, named Eric
─◆─

Live! Live! Live! But live with your heart, not your mind. Look not outside at nature and think how beautiful and magnificent. Look inside yourself and admire the extraordinary gifts that you have. You are perfect, for there is no such thing as imperfection! When you look inside, see only the perfection of you as you. There are no others quite like you.

You know, I spend lots of time with children who died very young, already feeling that they were imperfect. Strange, how you only see the person as perfect in that instant of birth. Every moment after that, you see imperfection. Remember that moment of birth and know that it is the Truth.

Tell your children they are perfect and, in telling them, begin to tell yourself. In your perfection, begin to live from your heart, for it will sing with joy when it knows of its perfection. Live! Thank you for listening and living the perfect you that you are.

---✧---

An old woman with straight white hair, named Ellen

---✧---

Death is but a doorway to life. I died an old woman who had lived fully but quietly. My life was uneventful but joyous. Many I knew as I aged feared Death as if it would steal their greatest treasure. All they thought about was Death; they even prepared all the details. Strange that the energy they put into their Death was greater than the energy that they put into their life.

What do you want to most teach us?

Worry not about Death; worry about how little you are living your life now. Stop focusing on what everyone else says and does. Ask only what gives you joy, what is your passion, how can you learn, and what matters to you, for nothing else is important. Live the answers to these questions. Answering them is not the purpose; living them is.

Death will come when you invite it, whether by thought or choice. Steal away in that moment to life across time. Know that, as you live, you are loved by many and all. Thank you.

---◆---

A young girl of seven, with brown hair in pigtails, named Eileen

---◆---

I died in a car accident. My daddy drove through a red light. I was killed by a truck. It hurt until I died.

What do you want to teach us?

Death is not final. I died in an instant, only so that my soul could leave my body and come here. Good thing, because my body could not go on. My daddy didn't die. He feels really sad and sometimes mad, because I died when he was driving. He and my mommy aren't as close anymore. They miss me, but they don't realize they also miss each other. They do not understand that I had to leave. It was my time to leave, because they needed to learn from my death. I died for them.

They are learning, but they are learning slowly. Once they learn, they can begin to live fully again. They must learn that all, even a child's death, has a purpose and we are all interconnected. You know, that truck driver had to learn, too.

Tell them that to live does not mean they will not experience sadness and pain, for pain is a teacher, too. It need not be the main teacher, though. Tell them to feel their pain and honor it as their teacher, but then let it go. Be free again on the journey that is their life, as they perceive it.

Tell them I am honored to have come into their lives to be their teacher. I learned, too, and now knowing that, will learn and grow. Tell them we will be together again. I surround them with my love. Thank you for carrying this message to them.

⊸✧⊷

An old Asian man in robes

⊸✧⊷

I am of all Time. I am the River. I am the Wind. I am the Air. I Am.

You are, too.

Time is endless and momentary. Be not consumed by time; be free of it. The time does not matter. Why do you make it so important? Choose and live. Do nothing more and worry not about time. Your worry steals the moment. You are left with nothing, for that which you thought mattered to you mattered less than that which you think matters next.

Just be in each moment until you choose to be in the next. Be the river that flows always, even when it is dry. Be the wind that whispers and wails as it dances across the Earth and time. Be the air, for it breathes life in every moment. Be you as the God-within that you are.

Be the life that you are, for if not, you are not. Know that you are loved.

---◇---

A group of children who died in a school bus accident

---◇---

Can we sing you our school song? Wait! One at a time!

All the children were happily talking when one took control, telling the others to wait. Who are you?

We are the children who died by the road. There were a lot of us. We were on our way home from school when the bus lost control. Everyone was screaming, and then some of us left the screaming.

Where did you go?

We went through a curtain and met a lot of people. Well, not people so much as energies like us. We recognized them, though. We were all met, and they took us to this place. It was so beautiful. Some of us felt real sad, so they took special care with them. Some still feel sad, so they are helping them understand. This place is awesome, though. You know, here we get to understand everything. We just do. We get to understand why we were there and why we left. It is pretty straightforward—it was time to leave.

What do you want to most teach us?

There is a time for everything, even leaving. Those who are left "behind," as you say, must know that. It was just time. Do not hold on to time that cannot be anymore. It was, so celebrate what it was, not what it may have been. Wake up! Use your time as you most want, then let it go. Let us go, for we must move on. If you let us go, you will go, too.

Know that our love will never be broken. Across time, we will be together again. Love will bring us there. Let us go so we can get there again. Thank you for sharing this. Tell them we are having a blast!

---◆---

A Native American Elder

---◆---

Who are you?

I am the Ancient One. You are wasting your life and your lives on a you that can never be, for it is them, not you. Why is it so hard for you to live your life? Do you not appreciate the gift that that life is?

My people lived as One. Our lives were not important, except as expressions of our lives as One. Do you understand the One that we all are? Can you not see that everything is interconnected? My pain is yours, your friend's joy is yours, and our world is but our thought as One.

How do you separate everything? How can it be done? Actually, it cannot, and that is your struggle. You are me. We are enemies and friends across lifetimes, for we cannot understand that there is no separation. All are equal as God.

See the differences and you become the differences. See the unity and act as One. You choose with your thoughts and your acts. Act as if you are acting upon yourself, even when what you do acts upon the Earth. There is no separation.

Strange, how you separate yourself even from you. Start with yourself, and when you see yourself as One with the

God-within—God as One, God-As-All—then you will see no separation with the Earth, world and universe.

You are God. Live as such! Feel my pain and joy, for I feel yours. I rejoice that I do. Let us rejoice together! Thank you for being you and listening to me.

A little boy, begging to be heard

I'm Jack. God *told me to tell my story. I was stolen by my father from my mother. My dad did it because he was mad at my mom, not because he wanted to be with me. We lived on the road, with no home, no friends and no life. Life was weird and empty, for it was all about keeping Mom from having something she wanted. I missed her, but didn't know how to find her. I told Dad I wanted to go home, but he said we couldn't, because the police would put us in jail. So I gave up thinking about finding her.*

What was the point, though? Life isn't about running away or going somewhere. We went everywhere but really went nowhere. We never stopped to enjoy the day or the sunshine. We drove through beautiful mountains and my dad would just complain about how tough it was to drive mountainous roads. We didn't make any friends, because Dad didn't want anyone to ask any questions. But knowing someone and asking questions matters. After a while, I just felt like I didn't matter, because I didn't matter to anyone, because no one knew me. Worst of all, I started not mattering to myself.

I realize now that many people we drove past are lonely and live lives "going" somewhere that is really nowhere.

In our non-physical experience of Self, we recognize all as "God." It is not that there is a more powerful "God."

Look around you. Do you spend time each day with those people that you love with your heart fully open? Do you tell them how important they are to you each day? Do you tell them that you love them every day?

What do you do with your time? Are you trying to "go" somewhere? Where? Why? Why is that place so important? Why is it more important than the place you are at? Are you stopping each day to see the flowers, feel the wind, listen to the river, and Be? Stop! Just Be! Just Be for me. Thanks.

⬦

An old woman

⬦

Live your life! Give it not away like it is worthless. Let no one take it from you, for it is yours to live. Know that there are no rules, no bounds and no limits. Imagine it and it will be! Rejoice! Exalt! Be!!!!! You are loved by all!

CHAPTER 7

The Simple Truth...
About Choice

In every moment of your life, you have choice. Every single one. What and how you choose defines the essence of who *you* are. Even choices you believe you did not make, you made by *not* making them.

Life is ultimately about nothing else but choosing to do with your time what *you* want to do. Strange, how we spend so much of our time convinced that we must do something that we really do not want to do. We do it because our parents would want us to do it, because we think there is some rule that says we must, or to be "accepted" by those around us.

Where is *your* joy? What do *you* feel excited about doing? Those are the questions you can choose to ask yourself. And, from the answers, you will live yourself into *your* life.

There is a responsibility that comes with choice. You delude yourself into believing that you do not have choices in order to try to avoid the responsibility and accountability for your own life.

You are accountable. It is *your* life. Look at it. Understand that, in any moment, you can choose differently or choose more of the same. Where is the joy? Live your joy and let others live theirs.

Choice is all-powerful, for it is the translation of thought into action. How you act and what you do reflect what you think. Know that to say one thing and do another fools no one. Your choice is what you *do*.

What will you *do* with your life? You are God—God-within. Know that you are all-powerful. Think it and it will be. All that is left for you, then, is to do it.

Choose and Live!

---◈---

I, the Messenger, as beings I have been across lifetimes

---◈---

We are here, for we have prepared to be here for lifetimes. We have lived in Truth, but not always fully lived our Truth. We made choices across lifetimes that kept us separate—like you, now—from the God-within that you are. Know that you are not alone in this separation, for the soul journey for all is about learning that there is no separation. We have finally learned that; now, we will finally live it.

We are here to invite you to join us. We have shared the universal Truths—the Simple Truth—so that you may more quickly learn what we have done over lifetimes. It is a sharing that unites us forever as the One that we are.

With this message, you have all the answers that you will ever need to know. All that is left for you to do is to choose. Choose you! Choose you as God—God-within!

For God is of life and, as you choose you, you will begin to live! We are so honored to be here with you at this time of choice. For, in but a moment, your choices will be different, your life changed, our world better, our universe expanded. Know how important your choices are to all and to us.

You are loved fully in every choice you make. You are only being asked to honor yourself as the God-within that you are and make your choices yourself for yourself. Worry not about others. All have abundance, and as you make your choices, you will teach them to make theirs.

CHAPTER 8

The Understanding

In the two years since I wrote *The Simple Truth About God*, I distributed the manuscript to all who were interested in reading it, and then self-published it so that it would be easily available worldwide. As the messenger of this Simple Truth, I honor my choice to walk this path by making choices that allow this work its greatest reach. I continue to do so with great love, as it reaches around the world.

Many who have read *The Simple Truth About God* have challenged me, some have approached me with questions, and others have remained silent in their own private experience. As you have read this book and now this chapter, know that your reaction and experience is about you. There is an enormous opportunity for you to learn. Observe your experience and you can learn about how you *love* yourself.

By adding this chapter, I have chosen to share the answers to some of the questions I have been repeatedly asked. I recognize that many of the concepts in this book are new and challenging to fundamentally accepted beliefs held by people across the world. I share these understandings with an open heart.

---❖---

Why is it called the "Simple" Truth?

---❖---

It is *simple,* because there is only one Truth shared in this book. That Truth is that each of us is God. After that Truth, everything else is a choice or a judgment.

Understand that everything is equal and neutral as a way to learn that there is no separation between oneself and God. One person may choose to learn through joy, while another may choose to learn through pain. Neither choice is "better" or "worse." The only difference is the experience the person will have, given one choice or another.

As God, we each choose all that we experience in our world. It is not that we choose pain. We choose how we will love ourselves. Every thought or word that diminishes us is one that creates pain. Every choice that honors us in joy calls forth greater joy. How we choose to love ourselves through our thoughts, words and actions calls forth different experiences, but that is all.

❖

Why does The Simple Truth About God use the word "God," rather than "Magnificent?"

❖

Mankind has chosen myriad ways of separating him or herself from all that he or she is. Even the term "God" has been used to describe that which mankind believes we are not. People have generally believed that God is the most magnificent being or energy that exists. That is why it matters that each reader understands the greatest Truth—that there is no other more magnificent than each of us as God. The word "God" captures that Truth and challenges readers to confront their choice of not celebrating their magnificence and perfection in all moments.

- ❖ -

How does mankind separate from living as God?

- ❖ -

We are masters at separating from the Truth that we are God. Throughout history, mankind has chosen to separate from self as God by choosing to see God as outside or to see God as something greater than self. This is the most fundamental choice of separation on earth, but not the only one.

We separate when we choose to judge ourselves or another as less or wrong because, by doing so, we are diminishing ourselves. When we see anything including angels, guides, Ascended Masters, spiritual leaders, gurus and spirits as greater than ourselves, we have separated by diminishing ourselves. When we blame an experience on an "unconscious" thought or choice, we separate from our responsibility for all that we create. When we hold on to the excuse that our present behavior or life is the result of our childhood experiences, we separate from our power as God. If we "put our intentions out to the universe," we diminish ourselves because we see a force in the universe as responsible or willing to do something for us we will not do for ourselves. If we see ourselves as greater as a "people" or "ethnic group," we separate. When we attribute our behavior or anxiousness to the cosmic alignment of universal energy, we are separating. When we blame a choice on something outside of ourselves, then we separate from our responsibility as God.

The experience of the acceptance of self as God is one of total presence to All that one is. We celebrate and experience our creation equally in all moments, whether it is a choice of pain or joy. We honor our choice to learn from that creation and understand that we can choose differently.

When we separate through our beliefs or actions, we make an all-powerful choice as God to deny that we "are" God. With that choice, we are no longer the experience of acceptance – peace and joy – but rather are the experience of the antithesis of acceptance – pain. We are no longer all-powerful; rather, we experience our powerlessness. The pain that we become is our choice and it is created, owned and empowered by us.

There is nothing we have perfected on earth more powerfully than this choice to separate from our Truth.

For thousands of years we have sought to find answers to our pain, hatred and lack. When we acknowledge our choice to separate from ourself as God, then we can begin to heal and gain understanding.

Many who read these words will say "I know that I am God." Spiritual movements and messengers have shared this Truth before, so some say, "I know that already." Others will say, "I know that I am part of God or part of a divine connection between all people and God." But saying that one knows they are God and living it are two different things.

Many I have come to know will tell me they know that they are God. But then they will share their judgment of others, blame forces outside of themselves for their lack, or share beliefs that something greater will provide for them if they are "good." Few know, even fewer live this Truth. That is why I am here now as a messenger of this Simple Truth.

—◇—

Is The Simple Truth About God about religion?

—◇—

The Simple Truth About God is about life. Religion has traditionally been mankind's sacred space for the exploration of self beyond the physical. It is one of few such places. Through religious institutions and spiritual experiences, mankind has allowed him or herself to conceive of God or Gods outside of oneself as being real.

In doing so, mankind has separated everyday life from that which is seen as sacred. With words of prayer, days of penance, rituals and tomes of religious stories, mankind has strengthened the barrier that separates mankind from the Truth that we *are* God.

The choice to follow a religious life is no better or worse than any other choice. If it honors one in joy to join others in a religious community, then it is a choice of selflove. If one chooses to follow the beliefs of a community because of fear of punishment from the community or eternal damnation, then it is not a choice that honors one in joy. If, through the beliefs of that community, one chooses to see oneself as less, then this, like all other choices that diminish, limits one's experience of self in this lifetime.

God is "of life." God is. It is not a question of whether we *are* God. It is only a question of how we choose to honor and live that Truth. Our lives are the expression of what we choose. How we live—*really* live—rather than calculating our lives and choices out of fear of loss, loneliness, rejection or shame, reflects how we choose to *be* God.

This book shares powerful, yet fully neutral understandings about life and how we each create our lives. It judges no choice as better than or worse than another choice, because all choices are equal, just different.

—◆—
Isn't it arrogant to say, "I am God?"
—◆—

Isn't it arrogant to say that we are not? Arrogance is false bravado. It diminishes all others around us, in order to fill our need to feel superior. If we say we are not that which we are because we believe that diminishing ourselves is an act of higher behavior, then are we not being arrogant in choosing to present ourselves as less, in order to feel greater?

The Simple Truth is not that YOU are God. It is that you are God, and so are your mother, neighbor, teacher, bus driver and government leader. No one person is superior to any other person. All people are equal.

Even our life choices as God are equal. One person is not superior to another because of how they live. One person as God chooses to harm another through abuse, criminal behavior or neglect. Another person chooses joyous dedication to others. Neither choice is better, just different. Both choices are ones made in order to learn that there is no separation between self and God. The difference, however, is the experience of those choices.

Each of those choices reflects itself in one's experience of self in joy, peace and love. A choice made from fear, lack or unworthiness manifests itself as pain, stress, anger or rage. Such a choice results in a diminished experience of All that we are as joy. On the other hand, a choice made in selflove results in an expansive experience of joy. All choices are honorable as ways of learning what it means to *be* God.

To know that you are God is not arrogant. To share that Truth with others is not arrogant. To be who we are is simply to *Be*.

---◇---

Is being "part of God" or "made in God's image" the same as "I am God?"

---◇---

A great many people ask me this question. It is so challenging for many people to conceive of themselves as God, and even more so to believe that there is no other greater God outside them. Some say to me that, if this book said that they were "of God," then they would be at peace.

How easy it is for so many to believe that mankind is "made in God's image," or is a "part of God," with the hope that this belief is true, rather than with the certainty that it is so. When I ask people to describe God, most people use words like love, compassion, goodness, light, oneness and perfection. Words like pain, hatred, anger, greed and darkness are reserved for something lesser, including mankind. It always strikes me as interesting where people draw the line. In other words, if one is a little angry with a friend out of love, then is that the "God part" of them because the anger is an act of love? Or does the "God part" begin when they live like a saint or monk?

It is greatly challenging for mankind to conceive of God as angry, stressed, vengeful, greedy and hurtful. But if man is "made in God's image" and man has all of those attributes, then God has them, too.

Some readers respond that this is not true, because it is man as "human" who corrupts the divine aspects of him or herself. It is interesting how people see man as powerful, in this instance, because, if man can corrupt that which is divine within, then man is more powerful than God. Yet, otherwise, man is powerless and less worthy, in comparison to God.

If we are "made in God's image" or a "part of God," then which part of us is God? In what mirror can we see the God that we are? The question always comes back to the same choice. How will we choose to experience that which we are as God? Even if we only allow ourselves to know ourselves in part as God, then why not choose to work from that part everyday, in every moment, and know that it is all-powerful? Every cell of us is all-powerful, so even if you choose to work with only one cell, you will be working with all that you are.

Know that when you choose to let go of all of your limitations concerning what part of God you are, or how you are made in God's image, then you will begin to experience your Truth. In an instant, you will see that those attributes of mankind which you judge as "bad" exist because man is God and does not acknowledge it.

When man denies he is God or sees himself as part of God, then, as God, man has chosen to separate from being God. The choice to see oneself as less or as powerless creates pain. The pain we experience is a choice, and, once we recognize that it is a choice, we can choose differently.

The instant mankind acknowledges the Truth, all those things we have chosen out of lack, self-abuse and self-hatred and which are expressed in pain, fear, stress and anger can change. With the decision to honor that these are our choices, we can then choose differently. By acknowledging our Truth, we can choose instead to love ourselves as magnificent and perfect, with unconditional acceptance.

What if the opposite of our fundamental Truth that God is separate is true? What if you and all *are* God?

What if all people knew it and acknowledged their choice to express all that they are through choices of selflove? Can you imagine our world, if we did so for even one day?

─◆─

Who is God-As-All?

─◆─

God-As-All, in *The Simple Truth About God*, is all that there is. Understand that each of us is a manifestation of All, in a momentary experience that we call self. That experience is momentary, because it is sustained only as a choice and changes instantly into another experience when we make a different choice.

The choice that sustains our experience is how we love ourselves. Every thought we have creates a structure within which we experience ourselves. Every word creates either an experience of celebration of self or one that diminishes self. Every action we take either honors us in joy or diminishes us.

Throughout this book, there are three terms for God—God, God-within and God-As-All. These terms embody one Truth—that there is no separation between self and God. God-within challenges you to understand that you are God and that there is no God outside of you. All is within.

God-As-All further acknowledges that All that you are aware of is a manifestation of yourself. There is no without. There is no separation, and there is nothing greater than you.

Many readers confuse God-As-All as being the embodiment of everything— mountains, oceans, planets and all forms of life. This choice to see an amalgam of all things as "God" is another choice of separation. It diminishes self as God, because self is seen as "part" of the "greater" whole.

Similarly, God-within is understood as the "part" of self that is God. This also separates self into "parts," with the belief that some part of us is God, while other parts are less or different. God-within, however, encompasses All, because there is nothing outside of self. We have no parts, just our experience of self as God manifested in millions of experiences.

Acknowledging all that you are matters, because you cannot "heal" anything unless you embrace it with love. When you acknowledge all that you are, you can heal, because there is nothing that you hold as separate, lesser or greater. The moment that you recognize yourself as God-As-All and acknowledge this as Truth, you understand that every moment of your life is about how you love yourself.

This understanding is important, because it is the key to *living* purposefully as God-As-All. Every moment of your life is one of choice and manifests the choice of how you love yourself. You can actively participate in learning from life how you are choosing to experience yourself as God.

For instance, when a co-worker or boss speaks to you with anger or judgment, it is a manifestation of your love for self. In that moment, you can ask, "What am I trying to learn?" The experience manifests the self-judgment or self-hatred in *your* heart. In that case, you can learn and choose to love yourself differently through your thoughts, words and actions. As you make different choices, you will manifest different experiences.

In the beginning of this book, God-As-All shares a powerful message. Understand that I, as God-As-All, share myself with you. Let this not confuse you. I am like you in body and life, except that I have come to know with absolute certainty that I am All that I am. In choosing to honor that Truth in the moment I chose to walk this path, I accepted all that I am as perfect.

With that acceptance, I allowed all that I am to be expressed as God-As-All. There is a purity of expression in the early passages of this book, because it is shared as you would express it as All that you are. In that moment, your words would not differ from mine.

I encourage you not to judge this experience of the voice of God-As-All as one of separation. Instead, I encourage you to see it as it is—the expression of everything, in one momentary sharing of Truth. You are God-As-All, just as I am. Choose to see this as Truth, and you will choose to see.

---◈---

If we are each All, then is there one God or many Gods?

---◈---

There is one God—one expression of self as All. Understand that All transcends self. The concept of self is one of separation. Acknowledging one's Truth as God calls forth the experience of one as All. When you know with certainty that you are God and you live that Truth, you experience others as you had only experienced yourself before. Thought is shared, pain is shared, knowing is instantaneous. Your choices, thoughts and words heal you and All. There is one experience of creation—yours.

Many are greatly challenged by the Truth that *they* are God. Understand that to think for one moment that you could *not be God* is to diminish your magnificence. It denies or judges you as less and calls forth the experience of limitation. You cannot know yourself as All until you let go of your fear and judgment about *being* All.

I have been asked by some readers, "If we are each God, creating all others in our world, then which came first, my thought of my neighbor or his thought of me?"

There is no time. There is only thought – the experience of self-awareness. In any moment, you have an awareness of self called other. That experience of the other is always yours because the other does not exist except for your choice as God to "be" in form. As God, you are always all creation. You just choose what you will notice of what always is.

Many believe that we *share* a consciousness. We do not share a consciousness. Consciousness is the experience of our choice to separate – the awareness of self. That awareness, by choice, is not shared, it is individuated. Our Truth is the same, not our experience of it. Because, as God, we have chosen across time to experience separation from self as All, our choice has resulted in the experience of individuation. Choosing to acknowledge and live your Truth will manifest in the transcendence of separation—Oneness. As God, there is no consciousness, just pure creation.

Acknowledging our Truth will not eliminate our individual experiences. It will eliminate the pain caused by the choice to deny our experience of All that we are.

It will allow us the joy of experiencing our Oneness as All that we are.

Man has sought to experience All or God by denying self. Many spiritual seekers and teachers have professed detachment from all that one experiences as self including the material world, seeing detachment as the key to enlightenment. This is not the experience of All; it is another experience of separation.

You cannot deny self in order to experience self as All. You must embrace self to know self as All. Choosing to deny yourself while believing that, by doing so, you are embracing something greater, diminishes everything.

Know that YOU are God. Your neighbor is God. Embrace yourself as God. Embrace All as self. Celebrate! Celebrate! Celebrate!

—◆—

What is prayer, if each of us is God?
It has always felt good to pray, and now I do not
know to whom I am praying.

—◆—

Prayer is an experience of communion with self. Prayer is and has been quite confused with the idea that it is a communion with "God-outside." The understanding that prayer is with yourself does not nullify its joy, unless the joy you experience is believing that someone else would do for you what you must do for yourself to experience all that you choose.

You have always been in communion with yourself; you just did not realize it. If you choose to pray, see prayer as expansion, and it will be. You are God, the most magnificent Being. Celebrate that Truth with love, so that you can experience your magnificence.

---◇---

What about when I am praying for another?

---◇---

There is no other outside of you. I know this sharing will challenge you, but others whom *you* experience are just momentary reflected images of light—your light—so that you can learn that *you* are God. Pray for another, and you are praying for yourself as another.

If you pray for another because you believe they are in pain, as God, you are experiencing your own pain manifested in the experience of self as another. Your reaction to the experience of another is an opportunity for you to learn. If you react with horror at a grave illness, you may want to look at your fear or judgment of pain. If you look at the experience as a tragedy, you may want to ask what can be learned by this choice. If you choose to pray as an act of selflove because the act of prayer gives you joy, you can more fully experience the healing of all.

Many people throughout the centuries have subscribed to the belief that group or mass prayer is more powerful than the prayer of one individual. The number of participants does not necessarily affect the power of prayer. If you believe prayer is more powerful with more participants than you alone, then, as God, you will experience prayer that way. If you believe it is just as powerful with only yourself, then, as God, you will experience it that way. It will be experienced as you choose because your belief system creates your reality.

- ◇ -

What about religious history and all the teachings that God is outside of us?

- ◇ -

If we look into history, we see our choices expressed in yesterday, as we understand time. The question is not whether yesterday's choices define today because they existed yesterday, but instead whether we will live today, as we know it, or live yesterday by holding on to those choices.

Over and over, mankind has chosen to see God as separate and outside. Fear is quite powerful, particularly when we honor it with choices and teachings that glorify it over other choices. I am not here to deny that mankind has chosen this path of separation in many of the world's most powerful religious traditions. It is true, and that is all.

I am here to share the Simple Truth that each of us is God. This sharing is not about religion; it is about life. For, in truth, most people who choose to follow the world's religious traditions are seeking to understand life. Each tradition asks, "What is it that we are here to do?" Some answer, "To suffer." Others, "To serve." Some, "To celebrate." And others, "To learn." None say, "To know that you *know*."

Many who choose to pursue greater "spiritual" understanding seek to know the "Truth." But most cling quite powerfully to yesterday's interpretation, rather than honoring it and letting it go, so that what they seek can manifest itself to them. Nothing changes unless we choose that it change. Traditions give us comfort and peace when we feel adrift. But they can do no more, because they do not honor the present moment, only the moment before.

"How would you know if God stood before you?"

You would only know if you chose to honor yourself as all-knowing and perfect—as God. Otherwise, you will rely on others to tell you and, in the process, diminish yourself. It's a contradiction. Religious teachings generally tell followers that God is separate, or, at most, a part of mankind. Yet, to know whether this is the truth, we have to fully honor our knowing, independent of that which we have previously relied upon. In that moment, we know. And that knowledge, if we choose, changes all else.

--◇--

Isn't it blasphemous to say, "I am God," when God is perfect and I am human?

--◇--

It is so easy for us to say that mankind, being human, has corrupted the God-within. Many believe God is "divine" and "perfect." "Perfection" is often defined as orderly, without fault, or characterized by grace, harmony and bliss. Through eyes of pain, we see our world in chaos, disorder and pain. Strangely, both accurately describe perfection, because each is perfectly all that it is. Perfect disorder is just that—perfect. The confusion arises with the judgment that one is intrinsically imperfect, instead of seeing that what is is perfect.

Mankind looks at the world, mankind's experience, and says this is *not* perfection, bliss or nirvana, because, if it were, pain would not exist. Yet mankind looks at nature and sees the natural world as perfect, almost without a thought about what "perfection" of the natural order would mean. Man accepts nature, as it is, as perfect, but reserves criticism and judgment for himself. It is strange how, in certain religious traditions, people believe that mankind is made in God's image, but then look in the mirror of life and say, "This is not God or what God looks like."

---◆---

How can I say that I am "perfect," when I get angry, judgmental or hateful? These are not the attributes of perfection.

---◆---

Perfection is not *a* state of being. It is *the* state of being. We often think of perfection as something we attain through hard work or certain behavior. But perfection is what is; all else is just an attempt to be something different because we judge our present choice as less.

Why do we categorize certain behavior as "better" than other behavior? All behaviors we judge as being less, such as anger, hate and jealousy, reflect our own pain and nothing more. We judge them because they "feel" bad. The consequence of our choice to not love ourselves is pain, depression, sadness and even experiences we turn upon others, such as anger and hate. It is our hearts that hurt, and we do not understand the power of acceptance as a healing force for our experience.

The struggle is that we cannot believe that pain, hatred and anger are "divine" experiences. In truth, they are the manifestation of our separation from the Truth that we are God. Acceptance of self as God manifests as peace. Living as God manifests as joy. We have come to know ourselves as pain and thereby that is our present experience of perfection – the state of our being. With a different choice, that experience changes.

Most people on Earth, however, are dissatisfied with themselves. It is the generally accepted way to be. All of that dissatisfaction calls forth greater and greater dissatisfaction, until mankind has little idea what would be satisfactory. Throughout time, cultures have developed standards to try to guide mankind in this search for "perfection." But few people, if any, have ever measured up. It is strange how hard so many have worked.

Know that those standards are just mankind's standards. They are not created or dictated by any external source. They are self-critical by their very nature and their attainment elusive.

The key to experiencing perfection as peace and joy is making the choice to know oneself as God and to live that Truth in each moment. To let go of our choice of separation, we must first accept that it was our choice. With acceptance, all healing occurs.

—◇—

How can "Hitler" be God?
Doesn't it blame the victims to assert that Hitler was created by the thoughts of those who believed a demon could exist so powerfully as to exterminate them?

—◇—

If one is not God, then none are so. If, at any moment, we judge another as being less than God, then there is no God. Each of us is All, and to judge another as less is to judge oneself as less.

Judgment is the mask we wear for our pain. Judgment is the very thing mankind most often reserves for God, and yet, it is the one thing mankind thoroughly practices in daily life. From the moment of birth, we hear words or thoughts of comparison. We define body types, behavior and actions as acceptable or not. Very early, children learn that everything, including themselves, is judged against all that is outside of them. The eyes of the world look outside, not inside.

Hitler was a man not unlike all men on Earth. He made choices, though, that have elicited the greatest anger from mankind that one could imagine. We see this man as a demon and, in doing so, see ourselves that way. What we do not understand is that we do not exist, except for the *thought* that we exist. To see Hitler as demonic is to see oneself as demonic. He is our belief in hatred, so powerful that it can destroy us, reflected as form.

Every thought creates. If we have thoughts of judgment, hatred, anger, fear or pain about ourselves, life, or our world, we create an experience of self in the world that is filled with that pain. There are *no* stray thoughts, and we will experience what we choose to believe.

Those who perished in the Holocaust are not to be "blamed." "Blame" suggests that choosing an experience of pain as a way to learn is less honorable than choosing joy. It is not so, just different. It is the *choice* that is to be understood.

Understand that one does not choose to die in a Holocaust. But we do choose in every moment how we will live. We choose with our thoughts, words and actions how we will love ourselves or diminish ourselves. It is interesting how much more readily people can accept their role in choosing joy than pain. But to accept one and not the other is to accept neither.

Everyday, we choose both. Every thought or word that diminishes us is a choice to lessen oneself. If you think you are too fat, unintelligent, fearful, angry, afraid or just "okay," you are diminishing yourself. Even if you believe you are not as good as you could be, but are striving to be better, you are seeing yourself as less.

If you listen to your everyday conversation, you will discover your pain. You will hear words of anger, self-deprecation and limited beliefs about yourself. In addition, every choice to fill your body with substances that are known to be harmful, such as alcohol, is choosing less. In many ways, we "kill" ourselves everyday and act as if that choice is nothing—a mere word or a drink.

In time, those choices manifest as pain in our bodies and our lives. In time, all of the repeated diminishing words accumulate in a torrent of self-hatred. We do not recognize it as such, but if we collected our words in buckets, those of pain and insult would overflow long before those of selflove. As the river in our hearts rages, we live the anger, hatred and fear in our lives. Everything around us—our friends, family, lives and world—become that which we are. The rage of Hitler was his and, as his, everyone's. The choice of those who perished was not to die at the hands of a demon. Rather, the choice was to hold onto pain, fear and rage, long before Hitler's manifestation.Understand that some held the pain across lifetimes because, once we choose a thought as God, it exists eternally unless we choose to release it. The choice to hold rage, hatred and anger expressed how those who perished "loved" themselves, for to hold pain and rage is to *be* it.

Hitler made choices with a grievous and life-changing impact on millions. It is hard to separate oneself from the depth of shared pain that has been passed down so powerfully ever since. It awakens in us the fear that one like Hitler could demonize us with such hatred.

Once this fear is awakened, most people do not let go of it and actually live it. Some have chosen never to separate from it. But let me ask, "How does a plant grow when its soil is moldy?" In time, it does not, for the mold will deny the plant adequate nutrients. If the gardener says, "The plant must always remember the mold, so I will leave the mold and just add new soil," then the plant will grow, but much more slowly. The mold will still choke out its growth.

Yet, for years, we have all done the same thing. We have held onto the mold or the pain with the belief that "remembering" is what will ensure that it will never be again. We have done this by passing down stories of hatred, anger and persecution to children, while vowing never to forget. We are the "gardeners," and all that this choice to remember ensures is that we will always know pain.

Hitler was a man living a life not unlike yours when he began to spiral down a path of powerful self-hatred. Consumed by that hatred, he turned it on others and found many people who became his followers, because they were equally experiencing pain. Hitler, his followers and those who perished were essentially manifesting the same experience—powerful self-hatred—as a way of learning about what it means to be God.

Through that experience, as horrific as it was, many who perished did learn the things they sought to teach through their message in this book. The souls of the Holocaust shared the Truth that the most powerful deterrent to mass destruction is selflove, because the choice to love oneself manifests experiences of self that are joyous and peaceful. If, with our thoughts, words and choices, we hold onto pain, fear and anger, then we are choosing to manifest the very same experiences we so seek to avoid.

Hitler, like his followers and those he impacted, made choices and lived out the experience of his choices. We hold him responsible for those choices with every word we speak of him. Yet we do not hold ourselves responsible for the choices we make each day. We look outside to God or fate and relinquish our responsibility. Once we begin to hold ourselves responsible, we begin to know that which we have demanded that Hitler know.

When we acknowledge that all is a choice and Hitler chose, just as we do everyday, then we know that we can choose differently, just as the despots, murderers and abusers of the world can. This is the most freeing acknowledgement. As God, we can choose differently. The world can change if we each choose joy rather than pain, selflove rather than self-hate, and knowing rather than fear.

All choices are equal. They are choices about how we love ourselves. The experiences of those choices differ. To choose from fear, pain or lack calls forth experiences of pain, fear and lack. To let go of fear, pain and lack and to choose from acceptance of self as perfect allows for the experience of all that we are—all joy, all peace, All.

When we love ourselves as perfect and magnificent, we let go of our choices to experience ourselves as pain and as victims. We are what we choose. Choose selflove and know joy.

Know that the Holocaust victims who shared their message in *The Simple Truth About God* did so for one reason. They learned that the greatest deterrent to mass destruction is selflove. Their cry was, "Love... Love... Love...." Millions came with this same message and the powerful desire to reach you.

The choice is yours. The experience is yours, too. What will you choose? Will you let go of your judgment and live?

---◆---

Does it matter whether or not I choose to know and live as God? How will it affect my life?

---◆---

Yes and no. Yes, because to know and live as God is to live. It matters whether you choose to honor that you are God because to choose not to do so separates you from the magnificence of all that you are.

And no, because you can choose to learn equally through joy or pain.

It is quite simple. As God, when you choose to deny that you are God, you choose as God to say that you are not that which God is; the experience of God, total acceptance of self as perfect, is peace. In living form, it is experienced as joy.

When you choose to see yourself as less than God, or to live thoughts, words and actions of separation from this Truth, you choose not to *be* God. The experience of mankind on earth to date has been the manifestation of the separation from this Truth, not the manifestation of its acceptance.

As God, you are limitless, all-powerful, all-knowing - the experience of all that is. In the moment of choice not to honor your Truth, you separate from this experience of your power, limitlessness and knowing. Your initial experience of the separation is feeling lost. You no longer feel that you know what to do. Life feels less certain. Soon you begin to feel fear, and with fear comes pain. In a short time, you know pain much more than joy and you build your life around the pain as you become it.

All healing work on earth today is done in the separation. It is working with the disruption of experience – most call it energetic vibration – that is caused by the choice to separate from this Truth.

Your essential experience as God is not one of vibration, it is one of stillness. That is why meditative experience helps individuals reach deeper understandings of their Truth. The meditative exercise quiets the disruption. However, it is ultimately ineffective at bringing people to peace because, at the same time it is quieting the "noise," the concurrent belief that one is not God is filling the person with disruption.

Choosing to know with certainty that you are God and living this Truth will change your life completely. The key is that you, like all others, have mastered separation from living as God. You have words that look outside for explanations for the experiences in your life. You have words filled with fear, self-diminishment and hate. You have walls behind which you hide from your fear that someone will discover you are not worthy. You have belief systems that you need to "become" something or "learn" something in order to reach a higher "level." You measure yourself against standards of performance, hoping to discover that you are "good enough."

Interestingly, even those who believe they already know they are God do not. Acknowledgement without choice is only acknowledgement. One does not know self as God until one chooses to *live* as God.

Are you willing to take responsibility for your life? Are you willing to stop blaming forces that you perceive as outside of you for your circumstances? Are you willing to stop engaging in conversations about yourself and others that are filled with pain and judgment? Only you can make these choices and only when you do will you know what it means that you are God.

When you do, your life will feel lighter, freer and joy-filled. It will not be the circumstances of your life that will determine your joy. It will just be the experience of you. It is magical and so much awaits you with the choice to know and live as God.

There is only one path to peace. It is the path of selflove. Selflove is the experience of total celebration of self as perfect and magnificent – the acceptance of self as God.

—◇—
What is selflove?
—◇—

Selflove is the total celebration of self. It is the experience of unconditional acceptance of self as All. Almost no one on the Earth knows this experience because, with thoughts of pain and fear, we have denied ourselves even a few moments of knowing the joy that we are. It is the key to knowing and experiencing all that we are.

Selflove is not a momentary "hug" of sorts. It is the experience of living in celebration of self with unconditional love. Very simply, it means choosing each day to say, "I love me." It means choosing words, thoughts and actions that are joyful for you and knowing that, as you do, you will honor all others, for they are experiences of you. It means looking at all of your paradigms or beliefs about self and choosing whether they honor you as perfect and magnificent, or whether they diminish your Truth.

What does it mean to believe that "you are becoming your full potential through growth and choices?" This paradigm is quite common and also very powerful. It chooses as its premise to see one's experience as linear, moving toward some undefined experience or goal, and assumes that one is not already All that they are. This assumption is based on the belief that one is less than All. Imagine that, as God, you believe this paradigm and its underlying assumptions. You will live these beliefs. Your life will be forever becoming your potential and always an experience of less than you are.

Imagine having a different paradigm that says, "I am All that I am." With this choice, you can rest from "becoming" and simply "Be." It is an act of selflove to recognize that you are perfect as you are and to celebrate that which you experience as you, in this moment. Even if it is a moment of pain or illness, choose to acknowledge your perfection and ask what you are to learn. Your acceptance of your choice to learn through pain will release your choice to learn that way. It will allow you to heal your heart and body.

To live in selflove, choose in each moment how you will love yourself. Listen to your words and your thoughts. Are they loving or disparaging? Are they based on fear of whether you will be accepted, or are they honoring of what you believe? Are you open with others about your beliefs? Do you live two lives—one publicly espousing universal platitudes of love and creation, and the other hiding your pain or thinking you are not good enough? Most people live such lives. Their greatest desire—to know themselves as divine—is stolen by their fear that they will be found out or known as not so.

Know that selflove is *thought as action*. The ultimate expression of how you love yourself is what you *do*, not what you say. Do you yearn to work in a career that others say is less lucrative or secure? Do you want to live away from your extended family because you love another part of the country, yet feel that leaving your family will be viewed as desertion? What have *you* chosen? Look at why you are choosing to continue a joyless experience when you yearn for something quite different. Loving yourself is the simplest act, but an *act* nonetheless. Look at your choices and ask whether they are joyful for you.

As you choose joy, you will then begin to know what love is. By choosing your joy, you will awaken the experience of selflove. In doing so, you will understand that love is not about the other. One cannot fully experience love from another until one can experience love for self. You must gift yourself first. You must choose to do for yourself what no other can do for you. Then, and only then, will you begin to know love.

Ask yourself everyday, "Does this give me joy?" If it does, then follow your joy. As you do so, you may at first experience the derision of others, or your own fear and even panic. Know that, for years, you have given away that which only you could hold—your knowing of what honors you in joy. Now, you can choose to accept the responsibility for that choice and experience that which you gave away so long ago. Stay with your joy and you will live a life you never imagined.

---⟡---

Isn't it selfish or egotistical to love oneself?

---⟡---

Why is it that, throughout centuries, we have focused all on the other, as if it is a "higher" or more "worthy" choice, than to focus on oneself? Isn't it ironic that everyone is being told to focus on one another in order to experience their own greatness? We have so many beliefs about how giving to others will return goodness to ourselves, or how selflessness is the highest experience of self. How many people do you know who are draining themselves of all energy and resources in giving to others, while inside they are in pain?

Denial of self as worthy is a choice. And, like all choices, it has consequences in the experience of that choice. Denying love for self because we believe it is selfish or egotistical is merely choosing to judge self as less than all others or others as less than self.

Selfishness is choosing something for self that one does not share with others. In truth, when we choose for self, we are choosing for all, because all others are momentary experiences of self that we call forth. It is not selfish to love oneself, it is more loving to do so.

All others in our world are but reflected thoughts of how we love ourselves. With unconditional selflove, we experience the healing of our pain—our judgment about self as "wrong" or "less than perfect." Through that healing, we no longer manifest others in our lives from pain, lack, fear or self-hatred. What we experience is that, as we love ourselves, everyone in our world changes, too. There is no greater act on behalf of all than to love self unconditionally as God—magnificent and perfect.

Equally so, it is not egotistical to love oneself. Egotism is mankind's experience of fear of self, not love or "inappropriate" love for self. Many people have chosen to seek strength through comparison with others, because they are afraid to acknowledge and accept all that they are as perfect. Taken to its extreme, this experience of comparison to demonstrate superiority is perceived as egotistical. It is a focus on one's "superiority," because one feels such lack within one's heart. One is afraid to accept oneself as perfect.

Mankind has chosen to judge almost everything as good or bad, better or worse, smarter or dumber, ugly or beautiful, and so on. All of these words and all other words of comparison are words of judgment—judgment of self as All. Remember that, as God, we are All, so that whomever we judge, we are judging ourselves. Egotism disappears when mankind accepts self as All and celebrates *everything*, not just that which mankind judges as "good" or "superior."

—◆—

How do we create pain?

—◆—

We are each All. There is no other outside. All that we experience as other is but a momentary reflected thought that we chose in order to experience self as God. Self as God is the energy called love. Love of self, when experienced, is joy. We are limitless joy.

When we choose with our thoughts, words, and actions to separate from acceptance of ourselves as God, we create pain. We not only create pain, but also become it. Our experience is the manifestation of our choices. When we separate, we choose to manifest ourselves as pain.

Most of us are almost completely neglectful of our words and explain away our choices. We use words as if they are meaningless, when they are actually all-powerful. For instance, to be self-deprecating is to diminish you. To speak about what is wrong, weak, or not good enough about your body is diminishing. To speak of others critically or with words of anger or pain is to speak of you that way.

Many people dream of living their lives differently but say that, because of responsibilities or expectations, they cannot do so. We make our own choices, and we are never prevented from making them differently. If we make our choices in fear or from a belief in lack, then we manifest an experience of less than all in our lives.

The more often we choose to experience ourselves as less, the more powerfully we lessen the experience of joy that we are by separating from our Truth. Ultimately, when our thoughts, words and actions are filled with ongoing self-hatred, fear or anger, we create significant pain in our bodies or our lives. Pain is thus the manifestation of our choices—choices that diminish and weaken the experience of joy that we are as All.

It is not complicated. That is why it is called the "Simple Truth." Our lives are just a powerful reflection of our choices. Choose your thoughts, words and actions with love for yourself, and watch your world reflect all the joy that you are. If it is pain that you have chosen, acknowledge the pain as an honorable choice and, with acceptance, ask what you are to learn from that experience. Then let go of that choice and choose anew.

Know that a choice once made or a thought once experienced exists eternally, until you choose, as God, to let it go. Everything is the eternal experience of self. Know that you can choose in any moment to honor and let go of your thoughts, words and choices of limitation. If you choose to do so, you can choose to experience more joy, more love and more freedom.

There is an easy, three-step process you can use to change your choices and manifest a different experience. At first, it may seem cumbersome, but you will soon find that it takes no more than five seconds.

Step One

First, we do not let go of anything unless we first embrace it with unconditional love and acceptance. If you try to *push* something away, it will not be released, because the choice to experience it was made as God.

To begin the process, say to yourself, *"I, (your name), as God, honor with great joy my choice to...."* For example, if you chose to react in anger to your spouse's behavior when she belittled you, then say, "I, (your name), as God, honor with great joy my choice to feel angry when my spouse belittled me."

Step Two

Next, say, *"But in this moment, I choose to release that choice and learn from it in perfection."* Now, as God, you will have released the original choice, word or thought that diminished you. By acknowledging that you will learn from the choice "in perfection," you have acknowledged that, in the right moment, you will know why you chose it. You do not need to spend countless hours figuring it out now.

In the example we are using, you will say, "But in this moment, I choose to release my choice to feel angry when my spouse belittled me and learn from it in perfection."

Step Three

Finally, to choose anew, say, *"In this moment and for all moments, I choose to learn through...."* Fill in this sentence with an affirmation of choice that serves you, such as "balance and joy," or "peace, joy and grace." In the example above, the closing can be, "But in this moment and for all moments, I choose to learn in peace, joy and acceptance of all."

Each time you do this three-step process, you will choose, as God, to shift the energetic experience you have chosen. What you hold in the spiritual manifests in the physical, so, over time, you will manifest greater peace and joy as you honor your choices, release them and choose joy.

However, understand that a life lived as God is not necessarily one lived without any pain or bumps. Your challenging experiences will lessen greatly with the choice to learn through joy. You will learn to acknowledge each experience with acceptance and live in grace. Honor your choices, but know that they are yours, and that you have the freedom to choose differently in any moment.

—◆—

What about thoughts and choices we make that are unconscious? Are we responsible for those as well?

—◆—

Conscious experience is all that we have. Many people confuse their neglect in choosing their words, thoughts or actions with "unconscious" behavior. Many live with so little awareness of self that they are surprised when someone else comments on how they behave.

Being awake is being totally *aware* of you. There is no one else who chooses all that *you* experience. Listen to your words. Do you hear them? Observe your choices. Your actions reflect your thoughts. If you strike out in anger, look at your self-judgment and pain. Experience your thoughts before you act upon them. As you have a thought, ask whether it will be of love if you express it. If not, do not...and choose another one.

You have *no* stray thoughts, words or actions. Each one is all-powerful. Acknowledge your Truth and then live it by living fully AWAKE.

--◇--

Why is it so hard for us to love ourselves? What are we afraid of?

--◇--

Many of us, if not almost all, are afraid of taking responsibility for our lives and world. As God, everything we are experiencing in our lives—lack in our marriage, inadequate sexual enjoyment, anger, frustration, fear, depression or just discontent—are *our* responsibility. This truth overwhelms many people, because it is so much easier to believe that something or someone else is responsible, or that in another lifetime or afterlife we will reap the reward for the pain we experience in this one.

Worthiness requires acknowledgement that, up until now, the lack has merely been our choice to see ourselves as less worthy than others. Over time, many people build lives around their pain. Conversations with friends and family support shared beliefs that we have this "pain" or "burden" to deal with. Many people even join in shared conversations about pain in order to be part of the accepted group.

Even more powerfully, many people create such burdens in order to relieve themselves of responsibility for living as they say they would otherwise choose to do. For instance, people will complain vociferously about how burdened they are by taking care of elderly parents and their needs. Those people will often say that they cannot pursue a new job or move away because of their parents. The truth is often that the individual is afraid to leave his job or hometown, not that there are no other options for the care of his parents.

On the Earth today, there is a dominant conversation about pain. It is often shared from the perspective that the pain is caused by factors or forces "outside" of us. Many people will complain about the tremendous stress in their lives, caused by their jobs, bosses, spouses, family and so on. Most people will say, "If only this one thing were different, then my life would be great."

To remove yourself from this conversation of pain, you must first acknowledge how you participate in it. You begin by identifying what pain you hold on to in your life. It can be anger at your parents over events that happened in childhood, frustration with the government, illnesses you have had and recovered from, or regrets about choices gone by.

Once you acknowledge how you are holding on to pain, you can choose to let it go. If you choose to let go of the pain, you must also choose to stop talking about it, using it as an excuse, or defining your life by it. For instance, a cancer survivor must choose to stop celebrating how long it has been since her last surgery or chemotherapy treatment.

Instead, choose to celebrate your life and joy, rather than your pain. How many of us jump to telephone friends to tell them about our bad news or the unfortunate news of another? How many people call friends to report the greatest moment of joy in their day or the good news of a mutual friend? Most of us make the first kind of call, few the second.

When we start to celebrate one another's joys rather than pains, we start to understand how powerfully we hold onto pain. At first, it may feel awkward to call to share news of another's joy. Some may even react with surprise at our having chosen to share such news. It is in those moments when we realize that, had we called to speak of another's misfortune, there would have been no surprise or momentary confusion.

We are also quite challenged in *living* a changed life. In other words, what do we have to give up to live in selflove? Do we have to give up our illnesses, which draw others to us in pity or dependence? Do we have to give up our excuses for why we cannot do something, such as full-time work? Do we have to give up our excuses about why we do not have friends or are not accepted? This list is endless, because we have all been masters at creating our reality and the support networks around us that confirm that reality.

If living a changed life brings fear into your heart, then you must choose whether you want to let go of those fears. If you do choose to let them go, then you can use the three-step process outlined earlier to do so. Acknowledge each choice in celebration and love. Let that choice go and choose anew. As you choose to let go, you will manifest choices or opportunities that will allow you to experience yourself differently. It will be your choices as actions—what you do rather than what you say—that will matter.

---◇---

Why does the focus of philanthropic efforts on providing for unmet needs create more unmet needs?

---◇---

Philanthropy that is focused on providing for unmet needs by donating resources from outside teaches the recipients that they are less powerful, thereby further diminishing their power. The message of the donation is that they are weak or weaker than others are. As recipients adopt that belief, their power diminishes and their needs ultimately increase. The "help" does not address the underlying choice of experiencing lack and the power of the individual, as God, to change that choice.

Awakening another to the knowing that he or she is God is no more or less powerful for the physically needy than for the physically abundant. Lack is of the heart, not the body. Feed both with the Simple Truth and both can be changed, if the person *chooses* to change.

It is not that philanthropic efforts are "bad" or "wrong," in and of themselves. The question is whether the choice to donate is one made in selflove or in judgment. If you choose to donate to a cause or to support a need because it is totally joyful for you to do so, then that is a choice made in selflove. If you choose to donate because you feel pity for the recipient, then that action will be the result of judgment. It will honor neither you nor the recipient.

In some countries, the wealthy receive tax breaks for donating to others. While there is self-gain associated with this choice, that does not change the fundamental question for the individuals who donate their wealth. The question is whether it is joyful for them to do so. If so, then the choice to donate is an act of selflove. If we donate because we feel guilty about our own abundance, then we are judgeing another's choice and diminishing our own. Selflove celebrates both choices equally.

―◆―
What is death?
―◆―

Death is one's physical expiration and spiritual reunion. Death is constant, because we die each day that we choose to live as less. Our cells, our self, our experience lessens in every moment we judge and choose to see life as limited. We all focus on the final expiration of the body, although we have died long before and hold on to the body as if we are nothing without it. It is interesting how we live as if the body is nothing, and yet, when faced with the end of our lives, we cling to it as if it were everything.

Focus on living. You have not yet lived. Do not delude yourself that you have, for that will only deny you the opportunity to choose to do so. *Living is the joyous, unconditional expression of self.* Tell the world, with every word, thought, and act you choose, that you are perfect and magnificent. Experience *you*, instead of dreaming about who you will be, or telling others who you are but acting differently. Live your life *now*. Let others live *their* lives. Share *you* with all and you will begin to live. Then you will finally know how you have been dying.

How does the soul die during a lifetime?

When we do not care for a flower, it will not grow. When we do not tend a fire, it will die out. You are a flower, a fire, All. You choose whether you will care for yourself with love, disdain, rebuke or even self-hatred. Don't think that your words of self-deprecation are mere words, for they are like acid to the flower and water to the fire. Every word, every thought and every act is either one that nourishes your experience or diminishes it.

Do not focus on the "soul" as an *aspect* of all that you are. Do not empower the soul with the belief that it is more, better, or divine in ways you are not. It only exists as a word, because you have chosen to name it as separate and thereby see it as so. You have separated self from All, with the choice to see mind, body and spirit as distinct.

You as All have choice in each moment to act in glorious love for self. You can nourish the flower and fuel the fire with selflove, or you can experience yourself as less. Neither choice is better, but, over time, one will result in pain and, like water on the fire, will ultimately extinguish the soul fire during your lifetime. This experience is rare but does occur.

It is not important whether you believe in a soul or not. It is only important that you know you have the choice to love yourself, and that it is that choice that will either allow you to experience all that you are or less of all that you are. Take time each day to thank yourself for all that you are as you experience yourself in joy.

---◇---

If we all chose in joy all of the time, won't the world be chaotic?

---◇---

Why is it assumed that, if one chooses joy, there will be less for another, or that choosing joy will result in chaos, while choosing pain results in order? Children choose joy all of the time. We teach them to choose pain. They are not chaotic, only joyful.

We experience all that we are when we choose selflove. We know that we always have what we want or need and allow it to be. This experience is one we cannot yet conceive; that we find it unimaginable marks the depth of our pain. Let us each choose to love ourselves and live into the knowing of what this will mean for ourselves and for our world.

To experience that which we have not yet experienced, we must let go of that which we know. What we know is just a choice to experience *some* of all that is. We have lived only a limited experience of self as All. We choose whether we will hold on to that limitation out of fear, or let it go, with the knowing that all will be.

---⋄---

How do people still living come to share their messages with you in this book?

---⋄---

Some readers have noticed that some of the voices captured in this book express their experience as taking place in a present lifetime, simultaneous to the one we are experiencing. The means of communication that allowed the sharing of messages in this book is love. This communication occurs after one has *left* the physical, just as easily as it does when one is *in* the physical.

While "flowing" this book, I never *thought* about writing anything in particular. It had never occurred to me that I would ever write a book about God, being God, or spiritual Truth. Two weeks prior to sitting down to write this book I had the knowing that I was to write a book with five chapters. I knew the chapter titles and the book title. I then merely allowed the voices to be shared by making time and typing what I "heard." I never judged the souls or their messages, although I knew some readers would do so in an effort to understand the message of this book.

While writing this book, I learned how we experience our Truth when we open our hearts. I also learned that time is an illusion. Some of those beings who shared present physical experiences have chosen to heal their pain while they now walk the Earth. In the moment of that choice their healing occurred, so that yours could also as you read their words.

Most of all, I learned that what is shared in any moment is perfect, for it is what we chose in order to know that we are God. As beings shared messages and love across time and space, I learned what it means to let go of all judgment and to accept the perfection of All.

Who are the "souls" who spoke to you in this book?

When the voice and soul visitations began, I experienced the souls as forms outside myself. I saw them, spoke to them through thought as sound and felt their love. It overwhelmed me. I even chose to share this book because I saw my role as just granting one small part of their request that I share their message.

In time, I came to know that, while they each had an experience of self as separate, what they were trying to teach is that we are All. They were teaching me that they, like me, were an expression of me as All. They presented themselves in a way I would notice, so that I would learn. They chose a powerful form with which to share their Truth—my Truth, *the* Truth.

We all are one expression of self. We are one expression of God-As-All. We speak in many beautiful and mystical ways about ourselves in order to reach through our pain with Truth. Most of the time, we acknowledge the mystery and beauty but dismiss the Truth. I chose not to dismiss the Truth, but to share it with all who choose to listen. Do not see this Truth as less because I acknowledge that it is mine...for, as mine, it is yours.

—◇—

Why should I believe you? What about all of the teachers, such as Jesus Christ, Buddha, the Dalai Lama and others who have walked the Earth sharing Truth?

—◇—

Friend, in these pages you have read about you but did not know it. I know it, and that is why I share it.

I do not ask that you believe *me*. Through this book, I am sharing nothing other than that you are *your* belief. If you believe that you are less—less worthy than another, less magnificent, less beautiful, less powerful or less perfect—then that is what you are. With this belief, you will experience yourself as less than All that you are. This choice is honorable and perfect, for it is yours. You will know who you are when you recognize that all that you *believe* is your choice of you.

Throughout history and even today, many have walked among you who have chosen to know they are divine, worthy, magnificent, knowing and even All. You have sought to understand them by dissecting their beliefs. Many of you have become more like them. I say to you that it is not *their* beliefs you need to understand to know you—it is *yours*.

It is very simple. I do not ask that you believe me. I ask that you *know* me as you would know yourself. I am like you, except that I have chosen to know All that I am. What do *you* choose to know?

Acknowledgements

This book was not written and published without the participation of All. Many have lovingly shepherded it to you, so that you can open your heart.

I thank Karen Pershing of A-1 Editing for gently and lovingly editing this book to allow the beauty of its words to flow more easily.

I sincerely thank Michele Ledoux for sharing her artistic gift so that this book breathes with life and beauty its truth.

There are a few family members and friends I would also like to acknowledge by name, because their effort, support and love guided this book and brought it into your hands. I share my deepest appreciation for my husband whose commitment to our family and choice to honor me helped me complete this work. I share particular thanks with Corey and Tyler, for teaching me the joy of being me as expressed in the sharing of this book. I thank Jodi for the purity of her being and her willingness to speak truthfully in all moments. Her editorial honesty guided me to speak more powerfully and clearly in the chapter entitled "The Understanding." Finally, I acknowledge my friend Chris, who read this book like no other. She touched my heart with her choice to read it and wrestle with the way it challenged her heart. I also thank all those readers, clients and friends who have read it and shared their comments and questions. I have opened my heart to answer them and now to thank them.

About the Author

Chris lives in the beautiful mountains of Colorado with her husband and children. She joyfully shares her life in love and friendship. She has chosen to share what she has learned with all who choose to understand what it means that we are God.

Her life completely changed when she experienced an extraordinary moment of discovery that she could hear and see souls across time. While educated as an attorney, she had been successfully running a marketing consulting business when she began to hear a voice sharing powerful messages about love, abundance, life, hate, joy and creation. Moved by the breadth of the messages and the love of the souls who also shared with her, she honored their call that she fulfill her life path in this lifetime—to walk the Earth as a messenger of the Simple Truth that we are all God.

In choosing to honor this path, she wrote both *The Simple Truth About God* and *Heart Songs: Messages for Parents from Children Across Time*. She came to know of her healing gifts—medical intuition, spiritual teaching, energetic healing and life-purpose messaging. She also co-founded, with Marilyn Innerfeld, *The Worldwide Center*.

In 2002, Chris was honored to be an Olympic Torchbearer in Colorado. She carried the torch with pride and joy, sharing the message to "light the fire within."

Chris now offers her teaching and healing services to individuals worldwide. She travels widely, presenting seminars and workshops, sharing insight about how we create our lives, and offering practical tools so that we can live powerfully as God in every moment.

About The Worldwide Center

The Worldwide Center is an international, personal and spiritual growth teaching center based in Evergreen, Colorado. The cornerstone of The Center's work is the *Expanded Living* program. The *Expanded Living* program is offered as self-empowerment workshops, one-on-one teaching sessions, teleclasses and meditation groups that share an expanded life vision, powerful self-help tools and alternative healing techniques. The Center's teaching is based on empowering those who seek to live an expanded life - one filled with joy, deep connection and great fulfillment - with practical tools to free their hearts and heal their bodies.

The Center's vision is to call forth world peace by teaching the power of selflove. The Center was co-founded in 1999 by Christine Lenick and Marilyn Innerfeld.

Other books published by Healing Arts Publishing include <u>Healing Through Love</u> by Marilyn Innerfeld.

To contact The Center:

The Worldwide Center
P.O. Box 4223
Evergreen, CO 80437
303-674-7704
www.expandedliving.net

As A Special Thanks
to the Reader

Begin to live an expanded life today! Visit us at www.expandedliving.net and take advantage of one of our offers as a special way to says thanks for sharing these teachings with us.

⟡

Free *Simple Truth About God* On-line Lessons

⟡

Get three *free* Living in Joy Lessons to begin to live fully today by registering as a reader at www.expandedliving.net. Register in <u>The Simple Truth About God</u> book area by clicking on the Living in Joy Lessons and you will receive your lessons instantly.

◆

Expanded Living Program Discounts

◆

The *Expanded Living* program is grounded in teaching an expanded life vision that each of us is magnificent and perfect - mankind's word for God. Looking at ourselves as magnificent and perfect is the most powerful moment of personal truth because it is a mirror for our choice of how we love ourselves. The *Expanded Living* program is offered either in workshops, teleclasses or one-on-one teaching sessions.

◆

Expanded Living Workshops and Teleclasses

◆

The *Expanded Living* Workshop is offered either live or via teleclass. One participant captured the power of the Center's work when she said, *"This course is amazing! The course content is truly revolutionary and will change people's lives in a significantly positive way."*

Get a special **10% reader's discount** on either a workshop or teleclass when you mention that you read one of the Center's books. This discount applies only if mentioned before the completion of the workshop or class.

Expanded Wellness or Expanded Life One-on-One Sessions

Over the telephone, from the comfort of your home, you can work one-on-one in private sessions with Christine Lenick or Marilyn Innerfeld. Using spiritual and medical intuitive gifts, Christine Lenick and Marilyn Innerfeld guide clients to heal their hearts and bodies. One time exploratory sessions are available and can be followed by ongoing one-on-one sessions helping you build a powerful and meaningful life tapestry filled with abundance, love and joy.

Take advantage of a special **10% discount** on your first session with either Christine Lenick or Marilyn Innerfeld when you mention that you read one of the Center's books.

Expanded Living E-Zine Newsletter

Stay in touch with the teachings of the Center by subscribing to the monthly *Expanded Living* E-zine at www.expandedliving.net.

Contact The Center Today:

The Worldwide Center
P.O. Box 4223
Evergreen, CO 80437
303-674-7704
www.expandedliving.net

Printed in the United States
15862LVS00001B/55-75